KRISHNAMURTI'S
JOURNAL

For a complete list, contact Krishnamurti Foundation Trust Ltd
or
Log on to www.kfoundation.org

KRISHNAMURTI'S JOURNAL

BY J. KRISHNAMURTI

Foreword by
Mary Lutyens

KRISHNAMURTI FOUNDATION TRUST LTD
2004

FOREWORD

In September 1973 Krishnamurti suddenly started keeping a journal. For nearly six weeks he made daily entries in a notebook. For the first month of that period he was staying at Brockwood Park, Hampshire, and for the rest of the time in Rome. He resumed the journal eighteen months later while in California.

Nearly every entry starts with a description of some natural scene which he knew intimately, yet in only three instances do these descriptions refer to the place in which he was actually staying. Thus, the first page of the first entry describes the grove in the park at Brockwood, but by the second page he is evidently in Switzerland in imagination. It is not until he is staying in California in 1975 that he again gives a description of his actual surroundings. For the rest, he is recalling places he has lived in, with a clarity that shows how vivid was his memory for natural scenery, arising from the acuteness of his observation. This journal also reveals to what an extent his teaching was inspired by his closeness to nature.

Throughout, Krishnamurti refers to himself in the third person as 'he', and incidentally he tells us something about himself which he had not done before.

Mary Lutyens

KRISHNAMURTI'S JOURNAL

Brockwood Park, Hampshire

That evening, while walking through the wood, we passed through the grove* near the big white house. Coming over the stile into the grove one felt immediately a great sense of peace and stillness. Not a thing was moving. It seemed sacrilegious to walk through it, to tread the ground; it was profane to talk, even to breathe. The great redwood trees were absolutely still; the American Indians call them the silent ones and now they were really silent. Even the dog didn't chase the rabbits. You stood still hardly daring to breathe; you felt you were an intruder, for you had been chatting and laughing, and to enter this grove not knowing what lay there was a surprise and a shock, the shock of an unexpected benediction. The heart was beating less fast, speechless with the wonder of it. It was the centre of this whole place. Every time you enter it now, there's that beauty, that stillness, that strange stillness. Come when you will and it will be there, full, rich and unnameable.

Any form of conscious meditation is not the real thing; it can never be. Deliberate attempt to meditate is not meditation. It must happen; it cannot be invited. Meditation is not the play of the mind nor of desire and pleasure. All attempt to meditate is the very denial of it. Only be aware of what you are thinking and doing and of nothing else. The seeing, the hearing, is the doing, without reward and punishment. The skill in doing lies in the skill of seeing, hearing. Every form of meditation leads inevitably to deception, to illusion, for desire blinds. It was a lovely evening and the soft light of spring covered the earth.

September 15, 1973

It is good to be alone. To be far away from the world and yet walk its streets is to be alone. To be alone walking up the path beside the rushing, noisy mountain stream full of spring water and melting snows is to be aware of that solitary tree, alone in its beauty. The loneliness of a man in the street is the pain of life; he's never alone, far away, untouched and vulnerable. To be full of knowledge is never to be alone and the activity of that knowledge breeds endless misery. The demand for expression, with its frustrations and pains, is that man who walks the streets; he is never alone. Sorrow is the movement of that loneliness.

That mountain stream was full and high with the melting snows and the rains of early spring. You could hear big boulders being pushed around by the force of on-rushing waters. A tall pine of fifty years or more crashed into the water; the road was being washed away. The stream was muddy, slate coloured. The fields above it were full of wild flowers. The air was pure and there was enchantment. On the high hills there was still snow, and the glaciers and the great peaks still held the recent snows; they will still be white all the summer long.

It was a marvellous morning and you could have walked on endlessly, never feeling the steep hills. There was a perfume in the air, clear and strong. There was no one on that path, coming down or going up. You were alone with those dark pines and the rushing waters. The sky was that astonishing blue that only the mountains have. You looked at it through leaves and the straight pines. There was no one to talk to and there was no chattering of the mind.

A magpie, white and black, flew by, disappearing into the woods. The path led away from the noisy stream and the silence was absolute. It wasn't the silence after the noise; it wasn't the silence that comes with the setting of the sun, nor that silence when the mind dies down. It wasn't the silence of museums and churches but something totally unrelated to time and space. It wasn't the silence that mind makes for itself. The sun was hot and the shadows were pleasant.

He only discovered recently that there was not a single thought during these long walks, in the crowded streets or on the solitary paths. Ever since he was a boy it had been like that, no thought entered his mind. He was watching and listening and nothing else. Thought with its associations never arose. There was no image-making. One day he was suddenly aware how extraordinary it was; he attempted often to think but no thought would come. On these walks, with people or without them, any movement of thought was absent. This is to be alone.

Over the snow peaks clouds were forming, heavy and dark; probably it would rain later on but now the shadows were very sharp with the sun bright and clear. There was still that pleas-ant smell in the air and the rains would bring a different smell. It was a long way down to the chalet.

September 16, 1973

At that time of the morning the streets of the small village were empty but beyond them the country was full with trees, meadows and whispering breezes. The one main street was lighted and everything else was in darkness. The sun would come up in about three hours. It was a clear starlit morning. The snow peaks and the glaciers were still in darkness and almost everyone was sleeping. The narrow mountain roads had so many curves that one couldn't go very fast; the car was new and being run in. It was a beautiful car, powerful with good lines. In that morning air the motor ran most efficiently. On the auto-route it was a thing of beauty and as it climbed it took every corner, steady as a rock. The dawn was there, the shape of the trees and the long line of hills and the vineyards; it was going to be a lovely morning; it was cool and pleasant among the hills. The sun was up and there was dew on the leaves and meadows.

He always liked machinery; he dismantled the motor of a car and when it ran it was as good as new. When you are driving, meditation seems to come so naturally. You are aware of the countryside, the houses, the farmers in the field, the make of the passing car and the blue sky through the leaves. You are not even aware that meditation is going on, this meditation that began ages ago and would go on endlessly. Time isn't a factor in meditation, nor the word which is the meditator. There's no meditator in meditation. If there is, it is not meditation. The meditator is the word, thought and time, and so subject to change, to the coming and going. It's not a flower that blooms and dies. Time is movement.

You are sitting on the bank of a river, watching the waters the current and the things floating by. When you are in the, water, there's no watcher. Beauty is not in the mere expression, it's in the abandonment of the word and expression, the canvas and the book.

How peaceful the hills, the meadows and these trees are: the whole country is bathed in the light of a passing morning. Two men were arguing loudly with many gestures, red in the face. The road runs through a long avenue of trees and the tenderness of the morning is fading.

The sea stretched before you and the smell of eucalyptus was in the air. He was a short man, lean and hard of muscle; he had come from a far-away country, darkened by the sun. After a few words of greeting, he launched into criticism. How easy it is to criticize without knowing what actually are the facts. He said: 'You may be free and live really all that you are talking about, and I am sure of this. But physically you are in a prison, padded by your friends. You don't know what is happening around you. People have assumed authority, though you yourself are not authoritarian.'

I am not sure you are right in this matter. To run a school or any other thing there must be a certain responsibility and it can and does exist without the authoritarian implication. Authority is wholly detrimental to co-operation, to talking things over together. This is what is being done in all the work that we are engaged in. This is an actual fact. If one may point out, no one comes between me and another.

'What you are saying is of the utmost importance. All that you write and say should be printed and circulated by a small group of people who are serious and dedicated. The world is exploding and it is passing you by.'

I am afraid again you are not fully aware of what is happening. At one time a small group took the responsibility of circulating what was being said, though they themselves printed the talks. Now, too, a small group has undertaken the same responsibility. Again, if one may point out, you are not aware of what is going on.

He made various other criticisms but they were based on assumptions and passing opinions. Without defending, one pointed out what was actually taking place. But—.

How strange human beings are.

The hills were receding and the noise of daily life was around one, the coming and the going, sorrow and pleasure. A single tree on a hillock was the beauty of the land. And deep down in the valley was a stream and beside it ran a railroad. You must leave the world to see the beauty of that stream.

That evening, walking through the wood there was a feeling of menace. The sun was just setting and the palm trees were solitary against the golden western sky. The monkeys were in the banyan tree, getting ready for the night. Hardly anyone used that path and rarely you met another human being. There were many deer, shy and disappearing into the thick growth. Yet the menace was there, heavy and pervading; it was all around you, you looked over your shoulder. There were no dangerous animals; they had moved away from there; it was too close to the sprawling town. One was glad to leave and walk back through the lighted streets. But the next evening the monkeys were still there and so were the deer and the sun was just behind the tallest trees; the menace was gone. On the contrary, the trees, the bushes and the small plants welcomed you. You were among your friends, you felt completely safe and most welcome. The woods accepted you and every evening it was a pleasure to walk there.

Forests are different. There's physical danger there, not only from snakes but from tigers that were known to be there. As one walked there one afternoon there was suddenly an abnormal silence; the birds stopped chattering, the monkeys were absolutely still and everything seemed to be holding its breath. One stood still. And as suddenly, everything came to life; the monkeys were playing and teasing each other, birds began their evening chatter and one was aware the danger had passed.

In the woods and groves where man kills rabbits, pheasants, squirrels, there's quite a different atmosphere. You are entering into a world where man has been, with his gun and peculiar violence. Then the woods lose their tenderness, their welcome, and here some beauty has been lost and that happy whisper has gone.

You have only one head and look after it for it's a marvellous thing. No machinery, no electronic computers can compare with it. It's so vast, so complex, so utterly capable, subtle and productive. It's the storehouse of experience, knowledge, memory. All thought springs from it. What it has put together is quite incredible: the mischief, the confusion, the sorrow, the wars, the corruptions, the illusions, the ideals, the pain and misery, the great cathedrals, the lovely mosques and the sacred temples. It is fantastic what it has done and what it can do. But one thing it apparently cannot do: change completely its behaviour in its relationship to another head, to another man. Neither punishment nor reward seems to change its behaviour; knowledge doesn't seem to transform its conduct. The me and the you remain. It never realizes that the me is the you, that the observer is the observed. Its love is its degeneration; its pleasure is its agony; the gods of its ideals are its destroyers. Its freedom is its own prison; it is educated to live in this prison, only making it more comfortable, more pleasurable. You have only one head, care for it, don't destroy it. It's so easy to poison it.

He always had this strange lack of distance between himself and the trees, rivers and mountains. It wasn't cultivated; you can't cultivate a thing like that. There was never a wall between him and another.

What they did to him, what they said to him never seemed to wound him, nor flattery [to touch him].

Somehow he was untouched. He was not withdrawn, aloof, but like the waters of a river. He had so few thoughts; no thoughts at all when he was alone. His brain was active when talking or writing but otherwise it was quiet and active without movement. Movement is time and activity is not.

This strange activity, without direction, seems to go on, sleeping or waking. He wakes up often with that activity of meditation; something of this nature is going on most of the time. He never rejected it or invited it. The other night he woke up, wide awake. He was aware that something like a ball of fire, light, was being put into his head, into the very centre of it. He watched it objectively for a considerable time, as though it were happening to someone else. It was not an illusion, something conjured up by the mind. Dawn was coming and through the opening of the curtains he could see the trees.

It is still one of the most beautiful valleys. It is entirely surrounded by hills, filled with orange groves. Many years ago there were very few houses among the trees and orchards but now there are many more; the roads are wider, more traffic, more noise, especially at the west end of the valley. But the hills and high peaks remain the same, un-touched by man. There are many trails leading to the high mountains and one walked endlessly along them. One met bears, rattle snakes, deer and once a bob cat (a lynx). The bob cat was there ahead, down the narrow trail, purring and rubbing him-self against rocks and the short trunks of trees. The breeze was coming up the canyon and so one could get quite close to him. He was really enjoying him-self, delighted with his world. His short tail was up, his pointed ears straight forward, his russet hair bright and clean, totally unaware that someone was just behind him about twenty feet away. We went down the trail for about a mile, neither of us making the least sound. It was really a beautiful animal, sprightly and graceful. There was a narrow stream ahead of us and wishing not to frighten him when we came to it, one whispered a gentle greeting. He never looked round, that would have been a waste of time, but streaked off, completely disappearing in a few seconds. We had been friends, though, for a considerable time.

The valley is filled with the smell of orange blossom, almost overpowering, especially in the early mornings and evening. It was in the room, in the valley and in every corner of the earth and the god of flowers blessed the valley. It would be really hot in the summer and that had its own peculiarity.

Many years ago, when one went there, there was a marvelous atmosphere; it is still there to a lesser degree. Human beings are spoiling it as they seem to spoil most things. It will be as before. A flower may wither and die but it will come back with its loveliness.

Have you ever wondered why human beings go wrong, become corrupt, indecent in their behaviour—aggressive, violent and cunning? It's no good blaming the environment, the culture or the parents. We want to put the responsibility for this degeneration on others or on some happening. Explanations and causes are an easy way out. The ancient Hindus called it karma, what you sowed you reaped. The psychologists put the problem in the lap of the parents. What the so-called religious people say is based on their dogma and belief. But the question is still there.

Then there are others, born generous, kind, responsible. They are not changed by the environment or any pressure. They remain the same in spite of all the clamour. Why?

Any explanation is of little significance. All explanations are escapes, avoiding the reality of 'what is'. This is the only thing that matters. The 'what is' can be totally transformed with the energy that is wasted in explanations and in searching out the causes. Love is not in time nor in analysis, in regrets and recriminations. It is there when desire for money, position and the cunning deceit of the self are not.

The monsoon had set in. The sea was almost black under the dark heavy clouds and the wind was tearing at the trees. It would rain for a few days, torrential rains, and it would stop for a day or so, to begin again. Frogs were croaking in every pond and the pleasant smell the rains brought filled the air. The earth was clean again and in a few days it became astonishingly green. Things grew almost under your eyes; the sun would come and all the things of the earth would be sparkling. Early in the morning there would be chanting and the small squirrels were all over the place. There were flowers everywhere, the wild ones and the cultivated, the jasmine, the rose and the marigold.

One day on the road that leads to the sea, while one walked under the palms and the heavy rain trees, looking at a thousand things, a group of children were singing. They seemed so happy, innocent and utterly unaware of the world. One of them recognized us, came smiling and we walked hand in hand for some time. Neither of us said a word and as we came near her house she saluted and disappeared inside. The world and the family are going to destroy her and she will have children too, cry over them and in the cunning ways of the world they will be destroyed. But that evening she was happy and eager to share it by holding a hand.

When the rains had gone, returning on the same road one evening when the western sky was golden, one passed a young man carrying a fire in an earthenware pot. He was bare except for his clean loincloth and behind him two men were carrying a dead body.

All were Brahmins, freshly washed, clean, holding themselves upright. The young man carrying the fire must have been the son of the dead man: they were all walking quite fast. The body was going to be cremated on some secluded sands. It was all so simple, unlike the elaborate hearse, loaded with flowers, followed by a long line of polished cars or mourners walking behind the coffin: the dark blackness of it all. Or you saw a dead body, decently covered, being carried at the back of a bicycle to the sacred river to be burnt.

Death is everywhere and we never seem to live with it. It is a dark, frightening thing to be avoided, never to be talked of. Keep it away from the closed door. But it is always there. The beauty of love is death and one knows neither. Death is pain and love is pleasure and the two can never meet; they must be kept apart and the division is the pain and agony. This has been from the beginning of time, the division and the endless conflict. There will always be death for those who do not see that the observer is the observed, the experiencer is the experienced. It is like a vast river in which man is caught, with all his worldly goods, his vanities, pains and knowledge. Unless he leaves all the things he has accumulated in the river and swims ashore, death will be always at his door, waiting and watching. When he leaves the river there is no shore, the bank is the word, the observer. He has left everything, the river and the bank. For the river is time and the banks are the thoughts of time; the river is the movement of time and thought is of it. When the observer leaves everything of which he is, then the observer is not. This is not death. It is the timeless. You cannot know it, for what is known is of time; you cannot experience it: recognition is made up of time. Freedom from the known is freedom from time. Immortality is not the word, the book, the image, you have put together. The soul, the 'me', the atman is the child of thought which is time. When time is not then death is not. Love is.

The western sky had lost its colour and just over the horizon was the new moon, young, shy and tender. On the road everything seemed to be passing, marriage, death, the laughter of children and someone sobbing. Near the new moon was a single star.

The river was particularly beautiful this morning; the sun was just coming over the trees and the village hidden among them. The air was very still and there was not a ripple on the water. It would get quite warm during the day but now it was rather cool and a solitary monkey was sitting in the sun. It was always there by itself, big and heavy. During the day it disappeared and turned up early in the morning on the top of the tamarind tree; when it got warm the tree seemed to swallow it. The golden green flycatchers were sitting on the parapet with the doves, and the vultures were still on the top branches of another tamarind. There was immense quietness and one sat on a bench, lost to the world.

Coming back from the airport on a shaded road with the parrots, green and red, screeching around the trees, one saw across the road what appeared to be a large bundle. As the car came near, the bundle turned out to be a man lying right across the road, almost naked. The car stopped and we got out. His body was large and his head very small; he was staring through the leaves at the astonishingly blue sky. We looked up too to see what he was staring at and the sky from the road was really blue and the leaves were really green. He was malformed and they said he was one of the village idiots. He never moved and the car had to be driven round him very carefully. The camels with their load and the shouting children passed him without paying the least attention. A dog passed, making a wide circle. The parrots were busy with their noise. The dry fields, the villagers, the trees, the yellow flowers were occupied with their own existence.

That part of the world was under-developed and there was no one or organization to look after such people. There were open gutters, filth and crowding humanity and the sacred river went on its way. The sadness of life was everywhere and in the blue sky, high in the air, were the heavy-winged vultures, circling without moving their wings, circling by the hour, waiting and watching.

What is sanity and insanity? Who is sane and who is insane? Are the politicians sane? The priests, are they insane? Those who are committed to ideologies, are they sane? We are controlled, shaped, pushed around by them, and are we sane?

What is sanity? To be whole, non-fragmented in action, in life, in every kind of relationship—that is the very essence of sanity. Sanity means to be whole, healthy and holy. To be insane, neurotic, psychotic, unbalanced, schizophrenic, whatever name you might give to it, is to be fragmented, broken up in action and in the movement of relationship which is existence. To breed antagonism and division, which is the trade of the politicians who represent you, is to cultivate and sustain insanity, whether they are dictators or those in power in the name of peace or some form of ideology. And the priest! Look at the world of priesthood. He stands between you and what he and you consider truth, saviour, god, heaven, hell. He is the interpreter, the representative; he holds the keys to heaven; he has conditioned man through belief, dogma and ritual; he is the real propagandist. He has conditioned you because you want comfort, security, and you dread tomorrow. The artists and the intellectuals—are they sane? Or do they live in two different worlds—the world of ideas and imagination with its compulsive expression, wholly separate from their daily life of sorrow and pleasure?

The world about you is fragmented and so are you and its expression is conflict, confusion and misery. You are the world and the world is you. Sanity is to live a life of action without conflict. Action and idea are contradictory. Seeing is the doing and not ideation first and action according to the conclusion. This breeds conflict. The analyser himself is the analysed. When the analyser separates himself as something different from the analysed, he then begets conflict, and conflict is the area of the unbalanced. The observer is the observed and therein lies sanity, the whole, and with the holy is love.

It is good to wake up without a single thought, with its problems. Then the mind is rested; it has brought about order within itself and that is why sleep is so important. Either it brings about order in its relationship and action during the waking hours, which gives to the mind complete rest during sleep, or during sleep it will attempt to arrange its affairs to its own satisfaction. During the day there will again be disorder caused by so many factors, and during the hours of sleep mind will try to extricate itself from this confusion. Mind, brain, can only function efficiently, objectively, where there is order. Conflict in any form is disorder. Consider what the mind goes through every day of its life: the attempt at order in sleep and disorder during waking hours. This is the conflict of life, day in, day out. The brain can only function in security, not in contradiction and confusion. So it tries to find it in some neurotic formula but the conflict becomes worse. Order is the transformation of all this mess. When the observer is the observed there is complete order.

In the little lane that goes by the house, shaded and quiet, a little girl was sobbing her heart out, as only children can do. She must have been five or six, small for her age. She was sitting on the ground, tears pouring down her cheeks, and she could hardly breathe with her sobbing. He sat down with her and asked what had happened but she couldn't talk; sobbing took all her breath. She must have been struck or her favourite toy broken or something which she wanted denied by a harsh word. The mother came out, shook the child and carried her in. She barely looked at him for they were strangers.

The mother must have given her permission to go with a strabger, He walked often in the shady lane and the girl with her brother and sister would come out and greet him. Will they ever forget their hurts and their sorrows or will they gradually build for themselves escapes and resistances? To keep these hurts seems to be the nature of human beings and from this their actions become twisted. Can the human mind never be hurt, wounded? Not to be hurt is to be innocent. If you are not hurt you will naturally not hurt another. Is this possible? The culture in which we live does deeply wound the mind and heart. The noise and the pollution, the aggression and competition, the violence and the education—all these and more contribute to the agony. Yet we have to live in this world of brutality and resistance: we are the world and the world is us. What is the thing that is hurt? The image that each one has built about himself, that is what is hurt. Strangely these images all over the world are the same, with some modifications. The essence of the image you have is the same as of the man a thousand miles away. So you are that man or woman. Your hurts are the hurts of thousands; you are the other.

Is it possible never to be hurt? Where there is wound there is no love. Where there is hurt, then love is mere pleasure. When you discover for yourself the beauty of never being hurt, then only do all the past hurts disappear. In the full present the past has lost its burden.

He has never been hurt though many things happened to him, flattery and insult, threat and security. It is not that he was insensitive, unaware; he had no image of himself, no conclusion, no ideology. Image is resistance and when that is not, there is vulnerability but no hurt.

You may not seek to be vulnerable, highly sensitive, for that which is sought and found is another form of the same image. Understand this whole movement, not merely verbally, but have an insight into it. Be aware of the whole structure of it without any reservation. Seeing the truth of it is the ending of the image builder.

The pond was overflowing and there were a thousand reflections on it. It became dark and the heavens were open.

A woman was singing next door; she had a marvellous voice and the few who were listening to her were entranced. The sun was setting among the mango trees and palms, rich golden and green. She was singing some devotion-al songs and the voice was getting richer and mellower. Listening is an art. When you listen to classical western music or to this woman, sitting on the floor, you are either being romantic or there are remembrances of things past or thought with its associations swiftly changing your moods, or there are intimations of the future. Or you listen without any movement of thought. You listen out of complete quietness, out of total silence.

Listening to one's thought or to the blackbird on a branch or to what is being said, without the response of thought, brings about a wholly different significance from that which the movement of thought brings. This is the art of listening, listening with total attention: there is no centre which listens.

The silence of the mountains has a depth which the valleys have not. Each has its own silence; the silence among clouds and among trees is vastly different; the silence between two thoughts is timeless; the silence of pleasure and of fear are tangible. The artificial silence which thought can manufacture is death; the silence between noises is the absence of noise but it is not silence, as the absence of war is not peace. The dark silence of a cathedral, of the temple, is of age and beauty, especially constructed by man; there is the silence of the past and of the future, the silence of the museum and the cemetery. But all this is not silence.

The man had been sitting there on the bank of the beautiful river, motionless; he was there for over an hour. He would come there every morning, freshly bathed, he would chant in

Sanskrit for some time and presently he would be lost in his thoughts; he didn't seem to mind the sun, at least the morning sun. One day he came and began to talk about meditation. He did not belong to any school of meditation, he considered them useless, without any great significance. He was alone, unmarried and had put away the ways of the world long ago. He had controlled his desires, shaped his thoughts and lived a solitary life. He was not bitter, vain or indifferent; he had forgotten all these some years ago. Meditation and reality were his life. As he talked and groped for the right word, the sun was setting and deep silence descended upon us. He stopped talking. After a while, when the stars were very close to the earth, he said: 'That is the silence I have been looking for everywhere, in the books, among the teachers and in myself. I have found many things but not this. It came unsought, uninvited. Have I wasted my life in things that did not matter? You have no idea what I have been through, the fastings, the self-denials and the practices. I saw their futility long ago but never came upon this silence. What shall I do to remain in it, to maintain it, to hold it in my heart? I suppose you would say do nothing, as one cannot invite it. But shall I go on wandering over this country, with this repetition, this control? Sitting here I am conscious of this sacred silence; through it I look at the stars, those trees, the river. Though I see and feel all this, I am not really there. As you said the other day, the observer is the observed. I see what it means now. The benediction I sought is not to be found in the seeking. It is time for me to go.'

The river became dark and the stars were reflected on its waters near the banks. Gradually the noises of the day were coming to an end and the soft noises of the night began. You watched the stars and the dark earth and the world was far away. Beauty, which is love, seemed to descend on the earth and the things of it.

He was standing by himself on the low bank of the river; it was not very wide and he could see some people on the other bank. If the talk was loud he could almost hear them. In the rainy season the river met the open waters of the sea. It had been raining for days and the river had broken through the sands to the waiting sea. With the heavy rains it was clean again and one could swim in it safely. The river was wide enough to hold a long narrow island green with bushes, a few short trees and a small palm. When the water was not too deep cattle would wade across to graze on it. It was a pleasant and friendly river and it was particularly so on that morning.

He was standing there with no one around, alone, unattached and far away. He was about fourteen or less. They had found his brother and himself quite recently and all the fuss and sudden importance given to him was around him*. He was the centre of respect and devotion and in the years to come he would be the head of organizations and great properties. All that and the dissolution of them still lay ahead. Standing there alone, lost and strangely aloof, was his first and lasting remembrance of those days and events. He doesn't remember his childhood, the schools and the caning. He was told years later by the very teacher who hurt him that he used to cane him practically every day; he would cry and be put out on the veranda until the school closed and the teacher would come out and ask him to go home, otherwise he would still be on the veranda, lost. He was caned, this man said because he couldn't study or remember anything he had read or been told. Later the teacher couldn't believe that boy was the man who had given the talk he had heard.

He was greatly surprised and unnecessarily respectful. All

those years passed without leaving scars, memories, on his mind; his friendships, his affections, even those years with those two who had ill-treated him. Somehow none of these events, friendly or brutal, have left marks on him. In recent years a writer asked if he could recall all those rather strange events, how he and his brother were discovered and so on, and when he replied that he could not remember them and could only repeat what others had said, the man openly, with a sneer, stated that he was putting it on and pre-tending. He never consciously blocked any happening, pleasant or unpleasant, entering into his mind. They came, leaving no mark and passed away.

Consciousness is its content: the content makes up consciousness. The two are indivisible. There is no you and another, only the content which makes up consciousness as the 'me' and the not 'me'. The contents vary according to the culture, the racial accumulations, the techniques and capacities acquired. These are broken up as the artist, the scientist and so on. Idiosyncrasies are the response of the conditioning and the conditioning is the common factor of man. This conditioning is the content, consciousness. This again is broken up as the conscious and the hidden. The hidden becomes important because we have never looked at it as a whole. This fragmentation takes place when the observer is not the observed, when the experiencer is seen as different from the experience. The hidden is as the open; the observation—the hearing of the open—is the seeing of the hidden. Seeing is not analysing. In analysing there is the analyser and the analysed, a fragmentation which leads to inaction, a paralysis.

In seeing, the observer is not, and so action is immediate; there is no interval between the idea and action. The idea, the conclusion, is the observer—the seer separate from the thing seen. Identification is an act of thought and thought is fragmentation.

The island, the river and the sea are still there, the palms and the buildings. The sun was coming out of masses of clouds, serried and soaring to the heavens. In only loincloths the fishermen were throwing their nets to catch some measly little fishes. Unwilling poverty is a degradation. Late in the evening it was pleasant among the mangoes and scented flowers. How beautiful is the earth.

A new consciousness and a totally new morality are necessary to bring about a radical change in the present culture and social structure. This is obvious, yet the left and the right and the revolutionary seem to disregard it. Any dogma, any formula, any ideology, is part of the old consciousness; they are the fabrications of thought whose activity is fragmentation—the left, the right, the centre. This activity will inevitably lead to bloodshed of the right or of the left or to totalitarianism. This is what is going on around us. One sees the necessity of social, economic and moral change but the response is from the old conscious-ness, thought being the principal actor. The mess, the confusion and the misery that human beings have got into are within the area of the old consciousness, and without changing that profoundly, every human activity, political, economic and religious, will only bring us to the destruction of each other and of the earth. This is so obvious to the sane.

One has to be a light to oneself; this light is the law. There is no other law. All other laws are made by thought and so fragmentary and contradictory. To be a light to oneself is not to follow the light of another, however reasonable, logic, historical, and however convincing. You cannot be a light to yourself if you are in the dark shadows of authority, of dogma, of conclusion. Morality is not put together by thought; it is not the outcome of environmental pressure, it is not of yesterday, of tradition. Morality is the child of love and love is not desire and pleasure. Sexual or sensory enjoyment is not love.

High in the mountains there were hardly any birds, there were crows, there were deer and an occasional bear. The huge redwoods, the silent ones, were everywhere, dwarfing all other trees. It was a magnificent country and utterly peaceful, for no hunting was allowed. Every animal, every tree and flower was protected. Sitting under one of those massive redwoods, one was aware of the history of man and the beauty of earth. A fat red squirrel passed by most elegantly, stopping a few feet away, watching and wondering what you were doing there. The earth was dry, though there was a stream nearby. Not a leaf stirred and the beauty of silence was among the trees. Going slowly along the narrow path, round the bend was a bear with four cubs as large as big cats. They rushed off to crawl up trees and the mother faced one without a movement, without a sound. About fifty feet separated us; she was enormous, brown, and prepared. One immediately turned one's back on her and left. Each understood that there was no fear and no intention to hurt, but all the same one was glad to be among the protecting trees, squirrels and the scolding jays.

Freedom is to be a light to oneself; then it is not an abstraction, a thing conjured by thought. Actual freedom is freedom from dependency, attachment, from the craving for experience. Freedom from the very structure of thought is to be a light to oneself. In this light all action takes place and thus it is never contradictory. Contradiction exists only when that law, light, is separate from action, when the actor is separate from action. The ideal, the principle, is the barren movement of thought and cannot co-exist with this light; one denies the other. This light, this law, is separate from you; where the observer is, this light, this love, is not.

The structure of the observer is put together by thought, which is never new, never free. There is no 'how', no system, no practice. There is only the seeing which is the doing.

You have to see, not through the eyes of another. This light, this law, is neither yours nor that of another. There is only light. This is love.

He was looking out of the window on to the green rolling hills and dark woods with the morning sun on them. It was a pleasant and lovely morning, there were magnificent clouds beyond the woods, white with billowing shapes. No wonder the ancients said the gods had their abode among them and the mountains. All around there were these enormous clouds against a blue and dazzling sky. He had not a single thought and was only looking at the beauty of the world. He must have been at that window for some time and something took place, unexpected and uninvited. You cannot invite or desire such things, unknowingly or consciously. Everything seemed to withdraw and be giving space only to that, the unnameable. You won't find it in any temple, mosque or church or on any printed page. You will find it nowhere and whatever you find, it is not that.

With so many others in that vast structure near the Golden Horn (Istanbul) he was sitting next to a beggar with torn rags, head lowered, uttering some prayer. A man began to sing in Arabic. He had a marvellous voice, the entire dome and great edifice was filled with it, it seemed to shake the building. It had a strange effect on all those who were there; they listened to the words and to the voice with great respect and were at the same time enchanted. He was a stranger amongst them; they looked at him and then forgot him. The vast hall was filled and presently there was a silence; they went through their ritual and one by one they left. Only the beggar and he remained; then the beggar too left. The great dome was silent and the edifice became empty, the noise of life was far away.

If you ever walk by yourself high in the mountains among the pines and rocks, leaving every-thing in the valley far below you, when there is not a whisper among the trees and every thought has withered away, then it may come to you, the otherness. If you hold it, it will never come again; what you hold is the memory of it dead and gone. What you hold is not the real; your heart and mind are too small, they can hold only the things of thought and that is barren. Go further away from the valley, far away, leaving everything down there. You can come back and pick them up if you want to but they will have lost their weight. You will never be the same again.

After a long climb of several hours, beyond the tree line, he was there among rocks and the silence only mountains have; there were a few stunted and misshaped pines. There was no wind and everything was utterly still. Walking back, moving from rock to rock, he suddenly heard a rattler and jumped. A few feet away was the snake, fat and almost black. With the rattle in the middle of the coils, it was ready to strike. The triangled head with its forked tongue flickering in and out, its dark sharp eyes watching, it was ready to strike if he moved nearer. It had given a warning; it had done its duty and it was up to you if you came nearer. During all that half hour or more it never blinked, it stared at you; it had no eyelids. Uncoiling slowly, keeping its head and tail towards him, it began to move away in a U-shape and when he made a move to get nearer it coiled up instantly ready to strike. We played this game for a little while; it was getting tired and he left it to go its own way. It was a really frightening thing, fat and deadly.

You must be alone with the trees, meadows and streams. You are never alone if you carry the things of thought, its images and problems. The mind must not be filled with the rocks and clouds of the earth. It must be empty as the newly-madevessel. Then you would see something totally, something that has never been. You can't see this if you are there; you must die to see it. You may think you are the important thing in the world but you are not. You may have everything that thought has put together but they are all old, used and begin to crumble.

In the valley it was surprisingly cool and near the huts the squirrels were waiting for their nuts. They had been fed every day in the cabin on the table. They were very friendly and if you weren't there on time they began their scolding and the blue jays waited noisily outside.

It was a temple in ruins, with its roofless long corridors, gates, headless statues and deserted courtyards. It had become a sanctuary for birds and monkeys, parrots and doves. Some of the headless statues were still massive in their beauty; they had a still dignity. The whole place was surprisingly clean and one could sit on the ground to watch the monkeys and chattering birds. Once very long ago, the temple must have been a flourishing place with thousands of worshippers, with garlands, incense and prayer. Their atmosphere was still there, their hopes, fears and their reverence. The holy sanctuary was gone long ago. Now the monkeys disappeared as it was growing hot but the parrots and doves had their nests in the holes and crevices of the high walls. This old ruined temple was too far away for the villagers to further destroy it. Had they come they would have desecrated the emptiness.

Religion has become superstition and image-worship, belief and ritual. It has lost the beauty of truth; incense has taken the place of reality. Instead of direct perception there is in its place the image carved by the hand or the mind. The only concern of religion is the total transformation of man. And all the circus that goes on around it is nonsense. That's why truth is not to be found in any temple, church or mosque, however beautiful they are. Beauty of truth and the beauty of stone are two different things. One opens the door to the immeasurable and the other to the imprisonment of man; the one to freedom and the other to the bondage of thought. Romanticism and sentimentality deny the very nature of religion, nor is it a plaything of the intellect.

Knowledge in the area of action is necessary to function efficiently and objectively, but knowledge is not the means of efficiently and objectively, but knowledge is not the means of the transformation of man; knowledge is the structure of thought and thought is the dull repetition of the known, however modified and enlarged. There is no freedom through the ways of thought, the known.

The long snake lay very still along the dry ridge of the rice fields, lusciously green and bright in the morning sun. Probably it was resting or waiting for some careless frog. Frogs were being shipped then to Europe to be eaten as a delicacy. The snake was long and yellowish and very still; it was almost the colour of the dry earth, hard to see but the light of day was in its dark eyes. The only thing that was moving, in and out, was its black tongue. It could not have been aware of the watcher who was somewhat behind its head. Death was everywhere that morning. You could hear it in the village; the great sobs as the body, wrapped in a cloth, was being carried out; a kite was streaking down on a bird; some animal was being killed; you heard its agonizing cries. So it went on day after day: death is always everywhere, as sorrow is.

The beauty of truth and its subtleties are not in belief and dogma; they never are where man can find them for there is no path to its beauty; it is not a fixed point, a haven of shelter. It has its own tenderness whose love is not to be measured nor can you hold it, experience it. It has no market value to be used and put aside. It is there when the mind and heart are empty of the things of thought. The monk or the poor man are not near it, nor the rich; neither the intellectual nor the gifted can touch it. The one who says he knows has never come near it. Be far away from the world and yet live in it.

The parrots were screeching and fluttering around the tamarind tree that morning; they begin early their restless activity, with their coming and going. They were bright streaks of green with strong, red, curved beaks. They never seemed to fly straight but always zig-zagging, shrieking as they flew. Occasionally they would come to sit on the parapet of the veranda; then you could watch them, but not for long; they would be off again with their crazy and noisy flight. Their only enemy seemed to be man. He puts them in a cage.

September 28, 1973

The big black dog had just killed a goat; it had been punished severely and tied up and it was now whining and barking. The house had a high wall around it but somehow the goat had wandered in and the dog had chased and killed it. The owner of the house made amends for it, with words and silver. It was a large house with trees around it and the lawn was never completely green however much it was watered. The sun was cruelly strong and all the flowers and bushes had to be watered twice a day; the soil was poor and the heat of the day almost withered the greenery. But the trees had grown large and gave comforting shadows and you could sit there in the early morning when the sun was well behind the trees. It was a good place if you wanted to sit quietly and lose yourself in meditation, but not if you wanted to daydream or lose yourself in some satisfying illusion. It was too severe there in those shadows, too demanding, for the whole place was given over to that kind of quiet contemplation. You could indulge in your friendly fantasies but you would soon find out that the place did not invite the images of thought.

He was sitting with a cloth over his head, weeping; his wife had just died. He did not want to show his tears to his children; they too were crying, not quite understanding what had happened. The mother of many children had been unwell and lately very ill; the father sat at her bedside. He never seemed to go out, and one day, after some ceremonies, the mother was carried out. The house had strangely become empty, without the perfume that the mother had given to it, and it was never the same again for there was sorrow in the house now.

The father knew it; the children had lost someone foreverbut as yet they did not know the meaning of sorrow.

- 44 -

It is always there, you cannot just forget it, you cannot cover it up through some form of entertainment, religious or otherwise. You may run away from it but it will be there to meet you again. You may lose yourself in some worship, prayer or in some comforting belief but it will appear again, unbidden. The flowering of sorrow is bitterness, cynicism or some neurotic behaviour. You may be aggressive, violent and nasty in your conduct but sorrow is where you are. You may have power, position and the pleasures of money but it will be there in your heart, waiting and preparing. Do what you will you cannot escape from it. The love that you have ends in sorrow; sorrow is time, sorrow is thought.

The tree is cut down and you shed a tear; an animal is killed for your taste; the earth is being destroyed for your pleasure; you are being educated to kill, to destroy, man against man. The new technology and machines are taking over the toils of men but you may not end sorrow through the things that thought has put together. Love is not pleasure.

She came desperate in her sorrow; she talked, pouring out all the things she had been through, death, the inanities of her children, their politics, their divorces, their frustrations, bitterness and the utter futility of all life that had no meaning. She was not young any more; in her youth she had just enjoyed herself, had a passing interest in politics, a degree in economics and more or less the kind of life that almost everyone leads. Her husband had died recently and all sorrow seemed to descend upon her. She became quiet as we talked.

Any movement of thought is the deepening of sorrow. Thought with its memories, with its images of pleasure and pain, with its loneliness and tears, with its self-pity and remorse, is the ground of sorrow. Listen to what is being said. Just listen—not to the echoes of the past, to the overcoming of sorrow or how to escape from its torture—but listen with your heart, with your whole being to what is now being said. Your dependence and attachment have prepared the soil for your sorrow. Your neglect of the study of yourself and the beauty it brings have given nourishment to your sorrow; all your self-centred activities have led you to this sorrow. Just listen to what is being said: stay with it, don't wander off. Any movement of thought is the strengthening of sorrow. Thought is not love. Love has no sorrow.

The rains were nearly over and the horizon was flowing
with billowing white and golden clouds; they were soaring up
to the blue and green heavens. All the leaves of every bush
were washed clean and they were sparkling in the early morning sun. It was a morning of delight, the earth was rejoicing
and there seemed to be benediction in the air. High up in that
room you saw the blue sea, the river running into it, the palms
and the mangoes. You held your breath at the wonder of the
earth and the immense shape of the clouds. It was early, quiet
and the noise of the day had not yet begun; across the bridge
there was hardly any traffic, only a long line of bullock carts,
laden with hay. Years later buses would come with their pollution and bustle. It was a lovely morning, full of song and bliss.

The two brothers were driven in a car to a village nearby to
see their father whom they had not seen for nearly fifteen years
or more. They had to walk a little distance on an ill-kept road.
They came to a tank, a storage of water; all its sides had stone
steps leading down to the clear water. At one end of it there
was a small temple with a small square tower, quite narrow at
the top; there were many images of stone all round it. On the
veranda of the temple, overlooking the big pond, were some
people, absolutely still, like those images on the tower, lost in
meditation. Beyond the water, just behind some other houses,
was the house where the father lived. He came out as the two
brothers approached and they greeted him by prostrating fully,
touching his feet. They were shy and waited for him to speak,
as was the custom. Before he said anything he went inside to
wash his feet, as the boys had touched them.

He was a very orthodox Brahmanah, no one could touch him
except another Brahmanah, and his two sons had been

polluted by mixing with others who were not of his class and had eaten food cooked by non-Brahmanahs. So he washed his feet and sat down on the ground, not too close to his polluted sons. They talked for some time and the hour when food is eaten approached. He sent them away for he could not eat with them; they were no longer Brahmanahs. He must have had affection for them, for after all they were his sons whom he had not seen for so many years. If their mother were alive she might have given them food but certainly would not have eaten with her sons. They must have had a deep affection for their children but orthodoxy and tradition forbade any physical contact with them. Tradition is very strong, stronger than love.

The tradition of war is stronger than love; the tradition of killing for food and killing the so-called enemy denies human tenderness and affection; the tradition of long hours of labour breeds efficient cruelty; the tradition of marriage soon becomes a bondage; the traditions of the rich and the poor keep them apart; each profession has its own tradition, its own elite which breeds envy and enmity. The traditional ceremonies and rituals in the places of worship, the world over, have separated man from man and the words and gestures have no meaning at all. A thousand yesterdays, however rich and beautiful, deny love.

You cross over a rickety bridge to the other side of a narrow, muddy stream which joins the big wide river; you come to a small village of mud and sun-dried bricks. There are quantities of children, screaming and playing; the older people are in the fields or fishing, or working in the near-by town.

In a small dark room an opening in the wall is the window; no flies would come into this darkness. It was cool in there. In that small space was a weaver with a large loom; he could not read but was educated in his own way, polite and wholly absorbed in his labours. He turned out exquisite cloth of gold and silver with beautiful patterns. In whatever colour of cloth or silk he could weave into traditional patterns, the finest and the best. He was born to that tradition; he was small, gentle and eager to show his marvellous talent. You watched him, as he produced from silken threads the finest of cloths, with wonder and love in your heart. There was the woven piece of great beauty, born of long tradition.

It was a long yellowish snake crossing the road under a banyan tree. He had been for a long walk and was coming back when he saw the snake. He followed it, quite closely, up a mound; it peered into every hole; it was totally unaware of him, though he was almost on top of it. It was quite fat; there was a large bulge in the middle of its length. The villagers on their way home had stopped talking and watched; one of them told him that it was a cobra and that he had better be careful. The cobra disappeared into a hole and he resumed his walk. Intent on seeing the cobra again at the same spot, he returned the next day. There was no snake there but the villagers had put a shallow pot of milk, some marigolds and a large stone with some ashes on it and some other flowers. That place had become sacred and every day there would be fresh flowers; the villagers all around knew that that place had become sacred. He returned several months later to that place; there was fresh milk, fresh flowers and the stone was newly decorated. And the banyan was a little older.

The temple overlooked the blue Mediterranean; it was in ruins and only the marble columns remained. In a war it was destroyed but it was still a sacred sanctuary. One evening, with the golden sun on the marble, you felt the holy atmosphere; you were alone, with no visitors about and their endless chatter. The columns were becoming pure gold and the sea far below was intensely blue. A statue of the goddess was there, preserved and locked up; you could only see her at certain hours and she was losing the beauty of sacredness. The blue sea remained.

It was a nice cottage in the country with a lawn that had been rolled, mown and weeded for many a year. The whole place was well looked after, prosperous and joyful; behind the house was a small vegetable garden; it was a lovely place with a gentle stream running beside, making hardly a sound. The door opened and it was held back by a statue of the Buddha, kicked into place. The owner was totally unaware of what he was doing; to him it was a door-stop. You wondered if he would do the same with a statue he revered, for he was a Christian. You deny the sacred things of another but you keep your own; the beliefs of another are superstitions but your own are reasonable and real. What is sacred?

He had picked it up, he said, on a beach; it was a piece of sea-washed wood in the shape of a human head. It was made of hard wood, shaped by the waters of the sea, cleansed by many seasons. He had brought it home and put it on the mantelpiece; he looked at it from time to time and admired what the sea had done. One day, he put some flowers round it and then it happened every day; he felt uncomfortable if there were not fresh flowers every day and gradually that piece of shaped wood became very important in his life. He would allow no one to touch it except himself; they might desecrate it; he washed his hands before he touched it. It had become holy, sacred, and he alone was the high priest of it; he re-presented it; it told him of things he could never know by himself. His life was filled with it and he was, he said, unspeakably happy.

What is sacred? Not the things made by the mind or hand or by the sea. The symbol is never the real; the word 'grass' is not the grass of the field; the word 'god' is not god. The word never contains the whole, however cunning the description.

The word sacred has no meaning by it-self; it becomes sacred only in its relationship to something, illusory or real. What is real is not the words of the mind; reality, truth, cannot be touched by thought. Where the perceiver is, truth is not. The thinker and his thought must come to an end for truth to be. Then that which is, is sacred—that ancient marble with the golden sun on it, that snake and the villager. Where there's no love there is nothing sacred. Love is whole and in it there's no fragmentation.

Consciousness is its content; the content is consciousness. All action is fragmentary when the content of consciousness is broken up. This activity breeds conflict, misery and confusion; then sorrow is inevitable.

From the air at that height you could see the green fields, each separate from the other in shape, size and colour. A stream came down to meet the sea; far beyond it were the mountains, heavy with snow. All over the earth there were large, spreading towns, villages; on the hills there were castles, churches and houses, and beyond them were the vast deserts, brown, golden and white. Then there was the blue sea again and more land with thick forests. The whole earth was rich and beautiful.

He walked there, hoping to meet a tiger, and he did. The villagers had come to tell his host that a tiger had killed a young cow the previous night and would come back that night to the kill. Would they like to see it? A platform on a tree would be built and from there one could see the big killer and also they would tie a goat to the tree to make sure that the tiger would come. He said he wouldn't like to see a goat killed for his pleasure. So the matter was dropped. But late that afternoon, as the sun was behind a rolling hill, his host wished to go for a drive, hoping that they might by chance see the tiger that had killed the cow. They drove for some miles into the forest; it became quite dark and with the headlights on they turned back. They had given up every hope of seeing the tiger as they drove back. But just as they turned a corner, there it was, sitting on its haunches in the middle of the road, huge, striped, its eyes bright in the headlamps.

The car stopped and it came towards them growling and

the growls shook the car; it was surprisingly large and its long tail with its black tip was moving slowly from side to side. It was annoyed. The window was open and as it passed growling, he put out his hand to stroke this great energy of the forest, but his host hurriedly snatched his arm back, explaining later that it would have torn his arm away. It was a magnificent animal, full of majesty and power.

Down there on that earth, there were tyrants denying freedom to man, ideologists shaping the mind of man, priests with their centuries of tradition and belief were enslaving man; the politicians with their endless promises were bringing corruption and division. Down there man is caught in endless conflict and sorrow and in the bright lights of pleasure. It is all so utterly meaningless—the pain, the labour and the words of philosophers. Death and unhappiness and toil, man against man.

This complex variety, modified changes in the pattern of pleasure and pain, are the content of man's consciousness, shaped and conditioned in the culture in which it has been nurtured, with its religious and economic pressures. Freedom is not within the boundaries of such a consciousness; what is accepted as freedom is in reality a prison made somewhat liveable in through the growth of technology. In this prison there are wars, made more destructive by science and profit. Freedom doesn't lie in the change of prisons, nor in any change of gurus, with their absurd authority. Authority does not bring the sanity of order. On the contrary it breeds disorder and out of this soil grows authority. Freedom is not in fragments.

A non-fragmented mind, a mind that is whole is in freedom. It does not know it is free; what is known is within the area of time, the past through the present to the future. All movement is time and time is not a factor of freedom.

Freedom of choice denies freedom; choice exists only where there is confusion. Clarity of perception, insight, is the freedom from the pain of choice. Total order is the light of freedom. This order is not the child of thought for all activity of thought is to cultivate fragmentation. Love is not a fragment of thought, of pleasure. The perception of this is intelligence. Love and intelligence are inseparable and from this flows action which does not breed pain. Order is its ground.

It was quite cold at the airport so early in the morning; the sun was just coming up. Every-one was wrapped up and the poor porters were shivering; there was the usual noise of an airport, the roars of the jets, the loud chatter, the farewells and the take-off. The plane was crowded with tourists, business men and others going to the holy city, with its filth and teeming people. Presently the vast range of the Himalayas became pink in the morning sun; we were flying south-east and for hundreds of miles these immense peaks seemed to be hanging in the air with beauty and majesty. The passenger in the next seat was immersed in a newspaper; there was a woman across the aisle who was concentrating on her rosary; the tourists were talking loudly and taking photographs of each other and of the distant mountains; everyone was busy with their things and had no time to observe the marvel of the earth and its meandering sacred river nor the subtle beauty of those great peaks which were becoming rose-coloured.

There was a man further down the aisle to whom considerable respect was being paid; he was not young, seemed to have the face of a scholar, was quick in movement and cleanly dressed. One wondered if he ever saw the actual glory of those mountains. Presently he got up and came towards the passenger in the next seat; he asked if he might change places with him. He sat down, introducing himself, and asked if he might have a talk with us. He spoke English rather hesitantly, choosing his words carefully for he was not too familiar with this language; he had a clear, soft voice and was pleasant in his manners.

He began by saying he was most fortunate to be travelling on the same plane and to have this conversation. 'Of course I have heard of you from my youth and only the other day I heard your last talk, meditation and the observer. I am a scholar, a pundit, practising my own kind of meditation and discipline.'

The mountains were receding further east and below us the river was making wide and friendly patterns.

'You said the observer is the observed, the meditator is the meditation and there's meditation only when the observer is not. I would like to be informed about this. For me meditation has been the control of thought, fixing the mind on the absolute.'

The controller is the controlled, is it not? The thinker is his thoughts. Without words, images, thoughts, is there a thinker? The experiencer is the experience; without experience there's no experiencer. The controller of thought is made up of thought; he's one of the fragments of thought, call it what you will; the outside agency however sublime is still a product of thought; the activity of thought is always outward and brings about fragmentation.

'Can life ever be lived without control? It's the essence of discipline.'

When the controller is the controlled, seen as an absolute fact, as truth, then there comes about a totally different kind of energy which transforms what is. The controller can never change what is; he can control it, suppress it, modify it or run away from it but can never go beyond and above it. Life can and must be lived without control. A controlled life is never sane; it breeds endless conflict, misery and confusion.

'This is a totally new concept.'

If it may be pointed out, it is not an abstraction, a formula. There's only what is. Sorrow is not an abstraction; one can draw a conclusion from it, a concept, a verbal structure but it is not what is, sorrow. Ideologies have no reality; there is only what is. This can never be transformed when the observer separates himself from the observed.

'Is this your direct experience?'

It would be utterly vain and stupid if this were merely verbal structures of thought; to talk of such things would be hypocrisy.

'I would have liked to find out from you what is meditation but now there's no time as we are about to land.'

There were garlands on arrival and the winter sky was intensely blue.

As a young boy, he used to sit by himself under a large tree near a pond in which lotuses grew; they were pink and had a strong smell. From the shade of that spacious tree, he would watch the thin green snakes and the chameleons, the frogs and the watersnakes. His brother, with others, would come to take him home*.

It was a pleasant place under the tree, with the river and the pond. There seemed to be so much space, and in this the tree made its own space. Everything needs space. All those birds on telegraph wires, sitting so equally spaced on a quiet evening, make the space for the heavens.

The two brothers would sit with many others in the room with pictures; there would be a chant in Sanskrit and then complete silence; it was the evening meditation. The younger brother would go to sleep and roll over and wake up only when the others got up to leave. The room was not too large and within its walls were the pictures, the images of the sacred. Within the narrow confines of a temple or church, man gives form to the vast movement of space. It is like this everywhere; in the mosque it is held in the graceful lines of words. Love needs great space.

To that pond would come snakes and occasionally people; it had stone steps leading down to the water where grew the lotus. The space that thought creates is measurable and so is limited; cultures and religions are its product. But the mind is filled with thought and is made up of thought; its consciousness is the structure of thought, having little space within it.

But this space is the movement of time, from here to there, from its centre towards its outer lines of consciousness, narrow or expanding. The space which the centre makes for itself is its own prison. Its relationships are from this narrow space but there must be space to live; that of the mind denies living. Living within the narrow confines of the centre is strife, pain and sorrow and that is not living.

The space, the distance between you and the tree, is the word, knowledge which is time. Time is the observer who makes the distance between himself and the trees, between himself and what is. Without the observer, distance ceases. Identification with the trees, with another or with a formula, is the action of thought in its desire for protection, security. Distance is from one point to another and to reach that point time is necessary; distance only exists where there is direction, inward or outward. The observer makes a separation, a distance between himself and what is; from this grows conflict and sorrow. The transformation of what is takes place only when there is no separation, no time, between the seer and the seen. Love has no distance.

The brother died and there was no movement in any direction away from sorrow. This non-movement is the ending of time. It was among the hills and green shadows that the river began and with a roar it entered the sea and the endless horizons. Man lives in boxes with drawers, acres of them and they have no space; they are violent, brutal, aggressive and mischievous; they separate and destroy each other. The river is the earth and the earth is the river; each cannot exist without the other.

There are no ends to words but communication is verbal and non-verbal. The hearing of the word is one thing and the hearing of no word is another; the one is irrelevant, superficial, leading to in-action; the other is non-fragmentary action, the flowering of goodness. Words have given beautiful walls but no space. Remembrance, imagination, are the pain of pleasure, and love is not pleasure.

The long, thin, green snake was there that morning; it was delicate and almost among the green leaves; it would be there, motionless, waiting and watching. The large head of the chameleon was showing; it lay along a branch; it changed its colour quite often.

There is a single tree in a green field that occupies a whole acre; it is old and highly respected by all the other trees on the hill. In its solitude it dominates the noisy stream, the hills and the cottage across the wooden bridge. You admire it as you pass it by but on your return you look at it in a more leisurely way; its trunk is very large, deeply embedded in the earth, solid and indestructible; its branches are long, dark and curving; it has rich shadows. In the evening it is withdrawn into itself, unapproachable, but during the daylight hours it is open and welcoming. It is whole, untouched by axe or saw. On a sunny day you sat under it, you felt its venerable age, and because you were alone with it you were aware of the depth and the beauty of life.

The old villager wearily passed you by, as you were sitting on a bridge looking at the sunset; he was almost blind, limping, carrying a bundle in one hand and in the other a stick. It was one of those evenings when the colours of the sunset were on every rock, tree and bush; the grass and the fields seemed to have their own inner light. The sun had set behind a rounded hill and amidst these extravagant colours there was the birth of the evening star. The villager stopped in front of you, looked at those startling colours and at you. You looked at each other and without a word he trudged on. In that communication there was affection, tenderness and respect, not the silly respect but that of religious men. At that moment all time and thought had come to an end. You and he were utterly religious, uncorrupted by belief, image, by word or poverty.

You often passed each other on that road among the stony hills and each time, as you looked at one another, there was the joy of total insight.

He was coming, with his wife, from the temple across the way. They were both silent, deeply stirred by the chants and the worship. You happened to be walking behind them and you caught the feeling of their reverence, the strength of their determination to lead a religious life. But it would soon pass away as they were drawn into their responsibility to their children, who came rushing towards them. He had some kind of profession, was probably capable, for he had a large house. The weight of existence would drown him and although he would go to the temple often, the battle would go on.

The word is not the thing; the image, the symbol is not the real. Reality, truth, is not a word. To put it into words wipes it away and illusion takes its place. The intellect may reject the whole structure of ideology, belief and all the trappings and power that go with them, but reason can justify any belief, any ideation. Reason is the order of thought and thought is the response of the outer. Because it is the outer, thought puts together the inner. No man can ever live only with the outer, and the inner becomes a necessity. This division is the ground on which the battle of 'me' and 'not me' takes place. The outer is the god of religions and ideologies; the inner tries to conform to those images and conflict ensues.

There is neither the outer nor the inner but only the whole. The experiencer is the experienced. Fragmentation is insanity. This wholeness is not merely a word; it is when the division as the outer and inner utterly ceases. The thinker is the thought.

Suddenly, as you were walking along, without a single thought but only observing without the observer, you became aware of a sacredness that thought has never been able to conceive. You stop, you observe the trees, the birds and the passer-by; it is not an illusion or something with which the mind deludes itself. It is there in your eyes, in your whole being. The colour of the butterfly is the butterfly.

The colours which the sun had left were fading, and before dark the shy new moon showed itself before it disappeared behind the hill.

It was one of those mountain rains that lasts three or four days, bringing with it cooler weather. The earth was sodden and heavy and all the mountain paths were slippery; small streams were running down the steep slopes and labour in the terraced fields had stopped. The trees and the tea plantations were weary of the dampness; there had been no sun for over a week and it was getting quite chilly. The mountains lay to the north, with their snow and gigantic peaks. The flags around the temples were heavy with rain; they had lost their delight, their gay colours fluttering in the breeze. There was thunder and lightning and the sound was carried from valley to valley; a thick fog hid the sharp flashes of light.

The next morning there was the clear blue, tender sky, and the great peaks, still and timeless, were alight with the early morning sun. A deep valley ran down between the village and the high mountains; it was filled with dark blue fog. Straight ahead, towering in the clear sky was the second highest peak of the Himalayas. You could almost touch it but it was many miles away; you forgot the distance for it was there, in all its majesty so utterly pure and measureless. By late morning it was gone, hidden in the darkening clouds from the valley. Only in the early morning it showed itself and disappeared a few hours later. No wonder the ancients looked to their gods in these mountains, in thunder and in the clouds. The divinity of their life was in the benediction that lay hidden in these unapproachable snows.

His disciples came to invite you to visit their guru; you politely refused but they came often, hoping that you would change your mind or accept their invitation, becoming weary of their insistence. So it was decided that their guru would come with a few of his chosen disciples.

It was a noisy little street; the children played cricket there; they had a bat and the stumps were a few odd bricks. With shouts and laughter they played cheerfully as long as they could, only stopping for a passing car as the driver respected their play. They would play day after day and that morning they were particularly noisy when the guru came, carrying a small, polished stick.

Several of us were sitting on a thin mattress on the floor when he entered the room and we got up and offered him the mattress. He sat cross-legged, putting his cane in front of him; that thin mattress seemed to give him a position of authority. He had found truth, experienced it and so he, who knew, was opening the door for us. What he said was law to him and to others; you were merely a seeker, whereas he had found. You might be lost in your search and he would help you along the way, but you must obey. Quietly you replied that all the seeking and the finding had no meaning unless the mind was free from its conditioning; that freedom is the first and last step, and obedience to any authority in matters of the mind is to be caught in illusion and action that breeds sorrow. He looked at you with pity, concern, and with a flare of annoyance, as though you were slightly demented. Then he said, 'The greatest and final experience has been given to me and no seeker can refuse that.'

If reality or truth is to be experienced, then it is only a projection of your own mind. What is experienced is not truth but a creation of your own mind.

His disciples were getting fidgety. Followers destroy their teachers and themselves. He got up and left, followed by his disciples. The children were still playing in the street, somebody was bowled out, followed by wild clapping and cheers.

There is no path to truth, historically or religiously. It is not to be experienced or found through dialectics; it is not to be seen in shifting opinions and beliefs. You will come upon it when the mind is free of all the things it has put together. That majestic peak is also the miracle of life.

The monkeys were all over the place that quiet morning; on the veranda, on the roof and in the mango tree—a whole troop of them; they were the brownish red-faced variety. The little ones were chasing each other among the trees, not too far from their mothers, and the big male was sitting by himself, keeping an eye over the whole troop; there must have been about twenty of them. They were rather destructive, and as the sun rose higher they slowly disappeared into the deeper wood, away from human habitation; the male was the first to leave and the others followed quietly. Then the parrots and crows came back with their usual clatter announcing their presence. There was a crow that would call or whatever it does, in a raucous voice, usually about the same time, and keep it up endlessly till it was chased away. Day after day it would repeat this performance; its caw penetrated deeply into the room and somehow all other noises seemed to have come to an end. These crows prevent violent quarrels amongst themselves, are quick, very watchful and efficient in their survival. The monkeys don't seem to like them. It was going to be a nice day.

He was a thin, wiry man, with a well-shaped head and eyes that had known laughter. We were sitting on a bench overlooking the river in the shade of a tamarind tree, the home of many par-rots and a pair of small screech-owls which were sunning themselves in the early morning sun.

He said: 'I have spent many years in meditation, controlling my thoughts, fasting and having only one meal a day. I used to be a social worker but I gave it up long ago as I found that such work did not solve the deep human problem.

There are many others who are carrying on with such work but it is no longer for me. It has become important for me to understand the full meaning and depth of meditation. Every school of meditation advocates some form of control; I have practised different systems but somehow there seems to be no end to it.'

Control implies division, the controller and the thing to be controlled; this division, as all division, brings about conflict and distortion in action and behaviour. This fragmentation is the work of thought, one fragment trying to control the other parts, call this one fragment the controller or whatever name you will. This division is artificial and mischievous. Actually, the controller is the controlled. Thought in its very nature is fragmentary and this causes confusion and sorrow. Thought has divided the world into nationalities, ideologies and into religious sects, the big ones and the little ones. Thought is the response of memories experience and knowledge, stored up in the brain; it can only function efficiently, sanely, when it has security, order. To survive physically it must protect itself from all dangers; the necessity of outward survival is easy to understand but the psychological survival is quite another matter, the survival of the image that thought has put together. Thought has divided existence as the outer and the inner and from this separation conflict and control arise. For the survival of the inner, belief, ideology, gods, nationalities, conclusions become essential and this also brings about untold wars, violence and sorrow. The desire for the survival of the inner, with its many images, is a disease, is disharmony. Thought is disharmony. All its images, ideologies, its truths are self-contradictory and destructive.

Thought has brought about, apart from its technological achievements, both outwardly and inwardly, chaos and pleasures that soon become agonies. To read all this in your daily life, to hear and see the movement of thought is the transformation that meditation brings about. This transformation is not the 'me' becoming the greater 'me' but the transformation of the content of consciousness; consciousness is its content. The consciousness of the world is your consciousness; you are the world and the world is you. Meditation is the complete transformation of thought and its activities. Harmony is not the fruit of thought; it comes with the perception of the whole.

The morning breeze had gone and not a leaf was stirring; the river had become utterly still and the noises on the other bank came across the wide waters. Even the parrots were quiet.

October 9, 1973

You went by a narrow-gauge train that stopped at almost every station where vendors of hot coffee and tea, blankets and fruit, sweets and toys, were shouting their wares. Sleep was almost impossible and in the morning all the passengers got into a boat that crossed the shallow waters of the sea to the island. There a train was waiting to take you to the capital, through green country of jungles and palms, tea plantations and villages. It was a pleasant and happy land. By the sea it was hot and humid but in the hills, where the tea plantations were, it was cool and in the air there was the smell of ancient days, uncrowded and simple. But in the city, as in all cities, there was noise, dirt, the squalor of poverty and the vulgarity of money; in the harbour there were ships from all over the world.

The house was in a secluded part and there was a constant flow of people who came to greet him with garlands and fruit. One day, a man asked if he would like to see a baby elephant and naturally we went to see it. It was about two weeks old and its mother was nervous and very protective, we were told. The car took us out of town, past the squalor and dirt to a river with brown water, with a village on its bank; tall and heavy trees surrounded it. The elephant and the baby were there. He stayed there for several hours till the mother got used to him; he had to be introduced, was allowed to touch its long trunk and to feed her some fruit and sugar cane. The sensitive end of the trunk was asking for more, and apples and bananas went into her wide mouth. The newly-born baby was standing, waving her tiny trunk, between her mother's legs. She was a small replica of her huge mother.

At last the mother allowed him to touch her baby; its skin was not too rough and its trunk was constantly on the move, much more alive than the rest of it. The mother was watching all the time and her keeper had to re-assure her from time to time. It was a playful baby.

The woman came into the small room deeply distressed. Her son was killed in the war: 'I loved him very much and he was my only child; he was well educated and had the promise of great goodness and talent. He was killed and why should it happen to him and to me? There was real affection, love between us. It was such a cruel thing to happen.' She was sobbing and there seemed to be no end to her tears. She took his hand and presently she became quiet enough to listen.

We spend so much money on educating our children; we give them so much care; we become deeply attached to them; they fill our lonely lives; in them we find our fulfilment, our sense of continuity. Why are we educated? To become technological machines? To spend our days in labour and die in some accident or with some painful disease? This is the life our culture, our religion, has brought us. Every wife or mother is crying all over the world; war or disease has claimed the son or the husband. Is love attachment? Is it tears and the agony of loss? Is it loneliness and sorrow? Is it self-pity and the pain of separation? If you loved your son, you would see to it that no son was ever killed in a war. There have been thousands of wars, and mothers and wives have never totally denied the ways that lead to war. You will cry in agony and support, unwillingly, the systems that breed war. Love knows no violence.

The man explained why he was separating from his wife. 'We married quite young and after a few years things began to go wrong in every way, sexually, mentally, and we seemed so utterly unsuited to each other. We loved each other, though, at the beginning and gradually it is turning into hate; separation has become necessary and the lawyers are seeing to it.'

Is love pleasure and the insistence of desire? Is love physical sensation? Is attraction and its fulfilment love? Is it a commodity of thought? A thing put together by an accident of circumstances? Is it of companionship, kindliness and friendship? If any of these take precedence then it is not love. Love is as final as death.

There is a path that goes into the high mountains through woods, meadows and open spaces. And there is a bench before the climb begins and on it an old couple sit, looking down on the sunlit valley; they come there very often. They sit without a word, silently watching the beauty of the earth. They are waiting for death to come. And the path goes on into the snows.

The rains had come and gone and the huge boulders were glistening in the morning sun. There was water in the dry river-beds and the land was rejoicing once again; the earth was redder and every bush and blade of grass was greener and the deep-rooted trees were putting out new leaves. The cattle were getting fatter and the villagers less thin. These hills are as old as the earth and the huge boulders appear to have been carefully balanced there. There is a hill towards the east that has the shape of a great platform on which a square temple has been constructed. The village children walked several miles to learn to read and write; there was one small child, all by herself, with shining face, going to a school in the next village, a book in one hand and some food in the other. She stopped as we went by, shy and inquisitive; if she stayed longer she would be late for her school. The rice fields were startlingly green. It was a long, peaceful morning.

Two crows were squabbling in the air, cawing and tearing at each other; there was not enough foothold in the air, so they came down to the earth, struggling with each other. On the ground feathers began to fly and the fight began to be serious. Suddenly about a dozen other crows descended upon them and put an end to their fight. After a lot of cawing and scolding they all disappeared into the trees.

Violence is everywhere, among the highly educated and the most primitive, among the intellectuals and the sentimentalists.

Neither education nor organized religions have been able to tame man; on the contrary, they have been responsible for wars, tortures, concentration camps and for the slaughter of animals on land and sea. The more he progresses the more cruel man seems to become. Politics has become gangsterism, one group against another; nationalism has led to war; there are economic wars; there are personal hatreds and violence. Man doesn't seem to learn from experience and knowledge, and violence in every form goes on. What place has knowledge in the transformation of man and his society?

The energy that has gone into the accumulation of knowledge has not changed man; it has not put an end to violence. The energy that has gone into a thousand explanations of why he's so aggressive, brutal, insensitive, has not put an end to his cruelty. The energy which has been spent in analysis of the causes of his insane destruction, his pleasure in violence, sadism, the bullying activity, has in no way made man considerate and gentle. In spite of all the words and books, threats and punishments, man continues his violence.

Violence is not only in the killing, in the bomb, in revolutionary change through bloodshed; it is deeper and more subtle. Conformity and imitation are the indications of violence; imposition and the accepting of authority are an indication of violence; ambition and competition are an expression of this aggression and cruelty, and comparison breeds envy with its animosity and hatred. Where there's conflict, inner or outer, there is the ground for violence. Division in all its forms brings about conflict and pain.

You know all this; you have read about the actions of violence, you have seen it in yourself and around you and you have heard it. You have knowledge of all this and perhaps more, and yet violence has not come to an end. Why? The explanations and the causes of such behaviour have no real significance. If you are indulging in them, you are wasting your energy which you need to transcend violence. You need all your energy to meet and go beyond the energy that is being wasted in violence. Controlling violence is another form of violence, for the controller is the controlled. In total attention, the summation of all energy, violence in all its forms comes to an end. Attention is not a word, an abstract formula of thought, but an act in daily life. Action is not an ideology, but if action is the outcome of it then it leads to violence.

After the rains, the river goes around every boulder, every town and village and however much it is polluted, it cleanses itself and runs through valleys, gorges and meadows.

Again a well-known guru came to see him. We were sitting in a lovely walled garden; the lawn was green and well kept, there were roses, sweet peas, bright yellow marigolds and other flowers of the oriental north. The wall and the trees kept out the noise of the few cars that went by; the air carried the perfume of many flowers. In the evening, a family of jackals would come out from their hiding place under a tree; they had scratched out a large hole where the mother had her three cubs. They were a healthy looking lot and soon after sunset the mother would come out with them, keeping close to the trees. Garbage was behind the house and they would look for it later. There was also a family of mongooses; every evening the mother with her pink nose and her long fat tail would come out from her hiding place followed by her two kits, one behind the other, keeping close to the wall. They too came to the back of the kitchen where sometimes things were left for them. They kept the garden free of snakes. They and the jackals seemed never to have crossed each other, but if they did they left each other alone.

The guru had announced a few days before that he wished to pay a call. He arrived and his disciples came streaming in afterwards, one by one. They would touch his feet as a mark of great respect. They wanted to touch the other man's feet too but he would not have it; he told them that it was degrading but tradition and hope of heaven were too strong in them. The guru would not enter the house as he had taken a vow never to enter a house of married people. The sky was intensely blue that morning and the shadows were long.

'You deny being a guru but you are a guru of gurus. I have observed you from your youth and what you say is the truth which few will understand. For the many we are necessary, otherwise they would be lost; our authority saves the foolish. We are the interpreters. We have had our experiences; we know. Tradition is a rampart and only the very few can stand alone and see the naked reality. You are among the blessed but we must walk with the crowd, sing their songs, repeat the holy names and sprinkle holy water, which does not mean that we are entirely hypocrites. They need help and we are there to give it. What, if one may be allowed to ask, is the experience of that absolute reality?'

The disciples were still coming and going, uninterested in the conversation and indifferent to their surroundings, to the beauty of the flower and the tree. A few of them were sitting on the grass listening, hoping not to be too disturbed. A cultured man is discontented with his culture.

Reality is not to be experienced. There's no path to it and no word can indicate it; it is not to be sought after and to be found. The finding, after seeking, is the corruption of the mind. The very word truth is not truth; the description is not the described.

'The ancients have told of their experiences, their bliss in meditation, their super consciousness, their holy reality. If one may be allowed to ask, must one set aside all this and their exalted example?'

Any authority on meditation is the very denial of it. All the knowledge, the concepts, the examples have no place in meditation. The complete elimination of the meditator, the experiencer, the thinker, is the very essence of meditation.

This freedom is the daily act of meditation. The observer isthe past, his ground is time, his thoughts, images, shadows, are time-binding. Knowledge is time, and freedom from the known is the flowering of meditation. There is no system and so there is no direction to truth or to the beauty of meditation. To follow another, his example, his word, is to banish truth. Only in the mirror of relationship do you see the face of what is. The seer is the seen. Without the order which virtue brings, meditation and the endless assertions of others have no meaning whatsoever; they are totally irrelevant. Truth has no tradition, it cannot be handed down.

In the sun the smell of sweet peas was very strong.

We were flying at thirty-seven thousand feet smoothly and the plane was full. We had passed the sea and were approaching land; far below us was the sea and the land; the passengers never seemed to stop talking or drinking or flipping over the pages of a magazine; then there was a film. They were a noisy group to be entertained and fed; they slept, snored and held hands. The land was soon covered over by masses of clouds from horizon to horizon, space and depth and the noise of chatter. Between the earth and the plane were endless white clouds and above was the blue gentle sky. In the corner seat by a window you were widely awake watching the changing shape of the clouds and the white light upon them.

Has consciousness any depth or only a surface fluttering? Thought can imagine its depth, can assert that it has depth or only consider the surface ripples. Has thought itself any depth at all? Consciousness is made up of its content; its content is its entire frontier. Thought is the activity of the outer and in certain languages thought means the outside. The importance that is given to the hidden layers of consciousness is still on the surface, with-out any depths. Thought can give to itself a centre, as the ego, the 'me', and that centre has no depth at all; words, however cunningly and subtly put together, are not profound. The 'me' is a fabrication of thought in word and in identification; the 'me', seeking depth in action, in existence, has no meaning at all; all its attempts to establish depth in relationship end in the multiplications of its own images whose shadows it considers are deep. All the activities of thought have no depth; its pleasures, its fears, its sorrow are on the surface.

The very word surface indicates that there is some-thing below, a great volume of water or very shallow. A shallow or a deep mind are the words of thought and thought in itself is superficial. The volume behind thought is experience, knowledge, memory, things that are gone, only to be recalled, to be or not to be acted upon.

Far below us, down on the earth, a wide river was rolling along, with wide curves amid scattered farms, and on the winding roads were crawling ants. The mountains were covered with snow and the valleys were green with deep shadows. The sun was directly ahead and went down into the sea as the plane landed in the fumes and noise of an expanding city.

Is there depth to life, to existence at all? Is all relationship shallow? Can thought ever discover it? Thought is the only instrument that man has cultivated and sharpened, and when that's denied as a means to the understanding of depth in life, then the mind seeks other means. To lead a shallow life soon becomes wearying, boring, meaningless and from this arises the constant pursuit of plea-sure, fears, conflict and violence. To see the fragments that thought has brought about and their activity, as a whole, is the ending of thought. Perception of the whole is only possible when the ob-server, who is one of the fragments of thought, is not active. Then action is relationship and never leads to conflict and sorrow.

Only silence has depth, as love. Silence is not the movement of thought nor is love. Then only the words, deep and shallow, lose their meaning. There is no measurement to love nor to silence. What's measurable is thought and time; thought is time. Measure is necessary but when thought carries it into action and relationship, then mischief and disorder begin. Order is not measurable, only disorder is.

The sea and the house were quiet, and the hills behind them, with all the wild flowers of spring, were silent.

Rome *

It had been a hot, dry summer with occasional showers; the lawns were turning brown but the tall trees, with their heavy foliage, were happy and the flowers were blooming. The land had not seen such a summer for years and the farmers were pleased. In the cities it was dreadful, the polluted air, the heat and the crowded streets; the chestnuts were already turning slightly brown and the parks were full of people with children shouting and running all over the place. In the country it was very beautiful; there is always peace in the land and the small narrow river with swans and ducks brought enchantment. Romanticism and sentimentality were safely locked up in cities, and here deep in the country, with trees, meadows and streams, there was beauty and delight. There's a road that goes through the woods, and dappled shadows and every leaf holds that beauty, every dying leaf and blade of grass. Beauty is not a word, an emotional response; it is not soft, to be twisted and moulded by thought. When beauty is there, every movement and action in every form of relationship is whole, sane and holy. When that beauty, love, doesn't exist, the world goes mad.

On the small screen the preacher, with carefully cultivated gesture and word, was saying that he knew his saviour, the only saviour, was living; if he was not living, there would be no hope for the world. The aggressive thrust of his arm drove away any doubt, any inquiry, for he knew and you must stand up for what he knew, for his knowledge is your knowledge, your conviction.

The calculated movement of his arms and the driven word were substance and encouragement to his audience, which was there with its mouth open, both young and old, spell-bound and worshipping the image of their mind. A war had just begun and neither the preacher nor his large audience cared, for wars must go on and besides it is part of their culture.

On that screen, a little later, there was shown what the scientists were doing, their marvellous inventions, their extraordinary space control, the world of tomorrow, the new complex machines; the explanations of how cells are formed, the experiments that are being made on animals, on worms and flies. The study of the behaviour of animals was carefully and amusingly explained. With this study the professors could better understand human behaviour. The remains of an ancient culture were explained; the excavations, the vases, the carefully preserved mosaics and the crumbling walls; the wonderful world of the past, its temples, its glories. Many, many volumes have been written about the riches, the paintings, the cruelties and the greatness of the past, its kings and its slaves.

A little later there was shown the actual war that was raging in the desert and among the green hills, the enormous tanks and the low-flying jets, the noise and the calculated slaughter; and the politicians talking about peace but encouraging war in every land. The crying women were shown and the desperately wounded, the children waving flags and the priests intoning blessings.

The tears of mankind have not washed away man's desire to kill. Religions have not stopped war; on the contrary, they have encouraged it, have blessed the weapons of war, have divided people. Governments are isolated and cherish their insularity.

The scientists are supported by governments. The preacher is lost in his words and images.

You will cry, but educate your children to kill and be killed.

You accept it as the way of life; your commitment is to your own security; it is your god and your sorrow. You care for your children so carefully, so generously, but then you are so enthusiastically willing for them to be killed. They showed on the screen baby seals, with enormous eyes, being killed.

The function of culture is to transform man totally.

Across the river mandarin ducks were splashing and chasing each other and the shadows of the trees were on the water.

There is in Sanskrit a long prayer to peace. It was written many, many centuries ago by someone to whom peace was an absolute necessity, and perhaps his daily life had its roots in that. It was written before the creeping poison of nationalism, the immorality of the power of money and the insistence on worldliness that industrial-ism has brought about. The prayer is to enduring peace: May there be peace among the gods, in heaven and among the stars; may there be peace on earth, among men and four-footed animals; may we not hurt each other; may we be generous to each other; may we have that intelligence which will guide our life and action; may there be peace in our prayer, on our lips and in our hearts.

There is no mention of individuality in this peace; that came much later. There is only ourselves—our peace, our intelligence, our knowledge, our enlightenment. The sound of Sanskrit chants seems to have a strange effect. In a temple, about fifty priests were chanting in Sanskrit and the very walls seemed to be vibrating.

There is a path that goes through the green, shining field, through a sunlit wood and beyond. Hardly anyone comes to these woods, full of light and shadows. It is very peaceful there, quiet and isolated. There are squirrels and an occasional deer, shyly watchful and dashing away; the squirrels watch you from a branch and sometimes scold you. These woods have the perfume of summer and the smell of damp earth. There are enormous trees, old and moss-laden; they welcome you and you feel the warmth of their welcome. Each time you sit there and look up through the branches and leaves at the wonderful blue sky, that peace and welcome are waiting for you.

You went with others through the woods but there was

aloofness and silence; the people were chattering, indifferent and unaware of the dignity and grandeur of the trees; they had no relationship with them and so in all probability, no relationship with each other. The relationship between the trees and you was complete and immediate; they and you were friends and thus you were the friend of every tree, bush and flower on earth. You were not there to destroy and there was peace between them and you.

Peace is not an interval between the ending and beginning of conflict, of pain and of sorrow. No government can bring peace; its peace is of corruption and decay; the orderly rule of a people breeds degeneration for it is not concerned with all the people of the earth. Tyrannies can never hold peace for they destroy freedom: peace and freedom go together. To kill another for peace is the idiocy of ideologies. You cannot buy peace; it is not the invention of an intellect; it is not to be purchased through prayer, through bargaining. It is not in any holy building, in any book, in any person. No one can lead you to it, no guru, no priest, no symbol.

In meditation it is. Meditation itself is the movement of peace. It is not an end to be found; it is not put together by thought or word. The action of meditation is intelligence. Meditation is none of those things you have been taught or experienced. The putting away of what you have learnt and experienced is meditation. The freedom from the experiencer is meditation. When there is no peace in relationship, then there is no peace in meditation; it is an escape into illusion and fanciful dreams. It cannot be demonstrated or described. You are no judge of peace.

You will be aware of it, if it is there, through the activities of your daily life, the order, the virtue of your life.

Heavy clouds and mists were there that morning; it was

going to rain. It would take several days to see the blue sky again. But as you came into the wood, there was no diminishing of that peace and welcome. There was utter stillness and incomprehensible peace. The squirrels were hiding and the grasshoppers in the meadows were silent and beyond the hills and valleys was the restless sea.

The wood was asleep; the path through it was dark and winding. There was not a thing stirring; the long twilight was just disappearing and the silence of the night was covering the earth. The small gurgling stream, so insistent during the day, was conceding to the quietness of the coming night. Through the small opening among the leaves were the stars, brilliant and very close. Darkness of the night is as necessary as the light of day. The welcoming trees were withdrawn into themselves and distant; they were all around but they were aloof and unapproachable; they were asleep, not to be disturbed. In this quiet darkness, there was growth and flowering, gathering strength to meet the vibrant day; night and day were essential; both gave life, energy, to all living things. Only man dissipates it.

Sleep is very important, a sleep without too many dreams, without tossing about too much. In sleep many things happen in the physical organism, in the brain; the mind is the brain, the heart and the organism; they are all one, a unitary movement. To this whole structure sleep is also absolutely essential. In sleep, order, adjustment, and deeper perceptions take place. The quieter the brain the deeper is the insight. The brain needs security and order to function harmoniously, without any friction. Night provides it and during quiet sleep there are movements, states, which thought can never reach. Dreams are disturbance; they distort total perception. In sleep the mind rejuvenates itself.

But you might say dreams are necessary; if one doesn't dream one might go mad; they are helpful, revealing. There are superficial dreams, without much meaning; there are dreams that are significant and there is also a dreamless state. Dreams are the expression in different forms and symbols of our daily life. If there is no harmony, no order in our daily life of relationship, then dreams are a continuance of that disorder. The brain during sleep tries to bring about order out of this confusing contradiction. In this constant struggle between order and disorder the brain is worn out. But it must have security and order to function at all, and so beliefs, ideologies and other neurotic concepts become necessary. Turning night into day is one of those neurotic habits; the inanities that go on in the modern world after nightfall are an escape from the daytime of routine and boredom.

The total awareness of disorder in relationship both private and public, personal and distant, an awareness of 'what is' without any choice during conscious hours during the day, brings order out of disorder. Then the brain has no need to seek order during sleep. Then dreams are only superficial, without meaning. Order in the whole of consciousness, not merely at the conscious level, takes place when division between the observer and the observed ceases completely. 'What is' is transcended when the observer who is the past, who is time, comes to an end. The active present, the what is, is not in the bondage of time as the observer is.

During sleep, when the mind—the brain and the organism—has this total order, then only there is an awareness of that wordless state, that timeless movement. This is not some fanciful dream, an abstraction of escape. It is the very summation of meditation.

That is, the brain is active, waking or sleeping, but the constant conflict between order and disorder wears down the brain. Order is the highest form of virtue, sensitivity, intelligence. When there is this great beauty of order, harmony, the brain is not endlessly active; certain parts of it have to carry the burden of memory but that is a very small part; the rest of the brain is free from the noise of experience. That freedom is the order, the harmony, of silence. This freedom and the noise of memory move together; intelligence is the action of this movement. Meditation is the freedom from the known and yet operating in the field of the known. There is no 'me' as the operator. In sleep or awake this meditation goes on.

The path came slowly out of the woods and from horizon to horizon the sky was filled with stars. In the fields not a thing moved.

It is the oldest living thing on the earth. It is gigantic in proportion, in its height and vast trunk. Among other redwood trees, which were also very old, this one was towering over them all; other trees had been touched by fire but this one had no marks on it. It had lived through all the ugly things of history, through all the wars of the world, through all the mischief and sorrow of man, through fire and lightning, through all the storms of time, untouched, majestic and utterly alone, with immense dignity. There had been fires but the bark of these redwood trees was able to resist them and survive. The noisy tourists had not come yet and you could be alone with this great silent one; it soared up to the heavens as you sat under it, vast and timeless. Its very years gave it the dignity of silence and the aloofness of great age. It was as silent as your mind was, as still as your heart, and living without the burden of time. You were aware of compassion that time had never touched and of innocency that had never known hurt and sorrow. You sat there and time passed you by and it would never come back. There was immortality, for death had never been. Nothing existed except that immense tree, the clouds and the earth. You went to that tree and sat down with it and every day for many days it was a benediction of which you were only aware when you wandered away. You could never come back to it asking for more; there was never the more, the more was in the valley far below. Because it was not a man-made shrine, there was unfathomable sacredness which would never again leave you, for it was not yours.

In the early morning when the sun had not yet touched the tops of the trees, the deer and the bear were there; we watched each other, wide-eyed and wondering; the earth was common to us and fear was absent. The blue jays and the red squirrels would come soon; the squirrel was tame and friendly. You had nuts in your pocket and it took them out of your hand; when the squirrel had had enough the two jays would hop down from the branches and the scolding would stop. And the day began.

Sensuality in the world of pleasure has become very important. Taste dictates and soon the habit of pleasure takes hold; though it may harm the whole organism, pleasure dominates. Pleasure of the senses, of cunning and subtle thought, of words and of the images of mind and hand is the culture of education, the pleasure of violence and the pleasure of sex. Man is moulded to the shape of pleasure, and all existence, religious or otherwise, is the pursuit of it. The wild exaggerations of pleasure are the outcome of moral and intellectual conformity. When the mind is not free and aware, then sensuality becomes a factor of corruption which is what is going on in the modern world. Pleasure of money and sex dominate. When man has become a second-hand human being, the expression of sensuality is his freedom. Then love is pleasure and desire. Organized entertainment, religious or commercial, makes for social and personal immorality; you cease to be responsible. Responding wholly to any challenge is to be responsible, totally committed. This cannot be when the very essence of thought is fragmentary and the pursuit of pleasure, in all its obvious and subtle forms, is the principal movement of existence.

Pleasure is not joy; joy and pleasure are entirely different things; the one is uninvited and the other cultivated, nurtured; the one comes when the 'me' is not and the other is time-binding; where the one is the other is not. Pleasure, fear and vioence run together; they are inseparable companions. Learning from observation is action, the doing is the seeing.

In the evening when the darkness was approaching, the jays and the squirrels had gone to bed. The evening star was just visible and the noises of the day and memory had come to an end. These giant sequoias were motionless. They will go on beyond time. Only man dies and the sorrow of it.

It was a moonless night and the Southern Cross was clear over the palm trees. The sun wouldn't be up for many hours yet; in that quiet darkness all the stars were very close to the earth and they were sparklingly bright; they were a penetrating blue and the river was giving birth to them. The Southern Cross was by itself without any other stars around it. There was no breeze and the earth seemed to stand still, weary of man's activity. It was going to be a lovely morning after the heavy rains and there wasn't a cloud on the horizon. Orion had already set and the morning star was on the far horizon. In the grove, frogs were croaking in the nearby pond; they would become silent for a while and wake up and begin again. The smell of jasmine was strong in the air and in the distance there was chanting. But at that hour there was a breathless silence and its tender beauty was on the land. Meditation is the movement of that silence.

In the walled garden the noise of the day began. The young baby was being washed; it was oiled with great care, every part of it; special oil for the head and another for the body; each had its own fragrance and both were slightly heated. The small child loved it; it was softly cooing to itself and its fat little body was bright with oil. Then it was washed, not with soap but with a special scented powder. The child never cried, there seemed to be so much love and care. It was dried and tenderly wrapped in a clean white cloth, fed and put to bed to fall asleep immediately. It would grow up to be educated, trained to work, accepting the traditions, the new or old beliefs, to have children, to bear sorrow and the laughter of pain.

The mother came one day and asked, 'What is love? Is it care, is it trust, is it responsibility, is it pleasure between man and woman? Is it the pain of attachment and loneliness?'

You are bringing up your child with such care, with tireless energy, giving your life and time. You feel, perhaps unknowingly, responsible. You love it. But the narrowing effect of education will begin, will make it conform with punishment and reward to fit into the social structure. Education is the accepted means for the conditioning of the mind. What are we educated for—for endless work and to die? You have given tender care, affection, and does your responsibility cease when education begins? Is it love that will send him to war, to be killed after all that care and generosity? Your responsibility never ceases, which doesn't mean interference. Freedom is total responsibility, not only for your children but for all children on the earth. Is love attachment and its pain? Attachment breeds pain, jealousy, hatred. Attachment grows out of one's own shallowness, insufficiency, loneliness. Attachment gives a sense of being and identification with something, gives a sense of reality, of being. When that is threatened there is fear, anger, envy. Is all this love? Is pain and sorrow love? Is sensory pleasure love? Most fairly intelligent human beings know verbally all this and it is not too complicated. But they do not let all this go; they turn these facts into ideas and then struggle with the abstract concepts. They prefer to live with abstractions rather than with reality, with 'what is'.

In the denial of what love is not, love is. Don't be afraid of the word negation. Negate all that is not love, then 'what is' is compassion. What you are matters enormously for you are the world and the world is you. This is compassion.

Slowly the dawn was coming; in the eastern horizon there was a faint light, it was spreading and the Southern Cross began to fade. The trees took on their shape, the frogs became silent, the morning star was lost in the greater light and a new

day began. The flight of crows and the voices of man had begun but the blessings of that early morning were still there.

In a small boat on the quiet slow current of the river all the horizon from north to south, east to west was visible; there wasn't a tree or house that broke the horizon; there was not a cloud floating by. The banks were flat, stretching on both sides far into the land and they held the wide river. There were other small fishing boats, the fishermen huddled at one end with their nets out; these men were immensely patient. The sky and the earth met and there was vast space. In this measureless space the earth and all things had their existence, even this small boat carried along by the strong current. Around the bend of the river the horizons extended as far as the eye could see, measureless and infinite. Space became in-exhaustible. There must be this space for beauty and compassion. Everything must have space, the living and the dead, the rock on the hill and the bird on the wing. When there is no space there is death. The fishermen were singing and the sound of their song came down the river. Sound needs space. The sound of a word needs space; the word makes its own space, rightly pronounced. The river and the faraway tree can only survive when they have space; without space all things wither. The river disappeared into the horizon and the fishermen were going ashore. The deep darkness of the night was coming, the earth was resting from a weary day and the stars were on the waters. The vast space was narrowed down into a small house of many walls. Even the large, palatial houses have walls shutting out that immense space, making it their own.

A painting must have space within it even though it's put in a frame; a statue can only exist in space; music creates the space it needs; the sound of a word not only makes space: it needs it to be heard. Thought can imagine the extension between two points, the distance and the measure; the interval between two thoughts is the space that thought makes. The continuous extension of time, movement and the interval between two movements of thought need space. Consciousness is within the movement of time and thought. Thought and time are measurable between two points, between the centre and the periphery. Consciousness, wide or narrow, exists where there is a centre, the 'me' and the 'not me'.

All things need space. If rats are enclosed in a restricted space, they destroy each other; the small birds sitting on a telegraph wire, of an evening, have the needed space between each other. Human beings living in crowded cities are becoming violent. Where there is no space, outwardly and inwardly, every form of mischief and degeneration is inevitable. The conditioning of the mind through so-called education, religion, tradition, culture, gives little space to the flowering of the mind and heart. The belief, the experience according to that belief, the opinion, the concepts, the word is the 'me', the ego, the centre which creates the limited space within whose border is consciousness. The 'me' has its being and its activity within the small space it has created for itself. All its problems and sorrows, its hopes and despairs are within its own frontiers, and there is no space. The known occupies all its consciousness. Consciousness is the known. Within this frontier there is no solution to all the problems human beings have put together. And yet they won't let go; they cling to the known or invent the unknown, hoping it will solve their problems.

The space which the 'me' has built for itself is its sorrow and the pain of pleasure. The gods don't give you space, for theirs is yours. This vast, measureless space lies outside the measure of thought, and thought is the known. Meditation is the emptying of consciousness of its content, the known, the 'me'.

Slowly the oars took the boat up the sleeping river and the light of a house gave it the direction. It had been a long evening and the sunset was gold, green and orange and it made a golden path on the water.

October 24, 1973

Way down in the valley were the dull lights of a small village; it was dark and the path was stony and rough. The waving lines of the hills against the starlit sky were deeply embedded in darkness and a coyote was howling somewhere nearby. The path had lost its familiarity and a small scented breeze was coming up the valley. To be alone in that solitude was to hear the voice of intense silence and its great beauty. Some animal was making a noise among the bushes, frightened of attracting attention. It was quite dark by now and the world of that valley became deep in its silence. The night air had special smells, a blend of all the bushes that grow on the dry hills, that strong smell of bushes that know the hot sun. The rains had stopped many months ago; it wouldn't rain again for a very long time and the path was dry, dusty and rough. The great silence with its vast space held the night and every movement of thought became still. The mind itself was the immeasurable space and in that deep quietness there was not a thing that thought had built. To be absolutely nothing is to be beyond measure. The path went down a steep incline and a small stream was saying many things, delighted with its own voice. It crossed the path several times and the two were playing a game together. The stars were very close and some were looking down from the hill tops. Still the lights of the village were a long way off and the stars were disappearing over the high hills. Be alone, without word and thought, but only watching and listening. The great silence showed that without it, existence loses its profound meaning and its beauty.

To be a light to oneself denies all experience. The one who is experiencing as the experiencer needs experience to exist and, however deep or superficial, the need for it becomes greater. Experience is knowledge, tradition, and the experiencer separates himself to discern between the enjoyable and the painful, the comforting and the disturbing. The believer experiences according to his belief, according to his conditioning. These experiences are from the known, for recognition is essential, without it there's no experience. Every experience leaves a mark unless there's an ending to it as it arises. Every response to challenge is an experience but when the response is from the known, challenge loses its newness and vitality; then there is conflict, disturbance and neurotic activity. The very nature of challenge is to question, to disturb, to awaken, to understand. But when that challenge is translated into the past, then the present is avoided. The conviction of experience is the negation of inquiry. Intelligence is the freedom to inquire, to investigate the 'me' and the 'not me', the outer and the inner. Belief, ideologies and authority prevent insight which comes only with freedom. The desire for experience of any kind must be superficial or sensory, comforting or pleasurable, for desire, however intense, is the forerunner of thought and thought is the outer. Thought may put together the inner but it is still the outer. Thought will never find the new for it is old, it is never free. Freedom lies beyond thought. All the activity of thought is not love.

To be a light to oneself is the light of all others. To be a light to oneself is for the mind to be free from challenge and response, for the mind then is totally awake, wholly attentive. This attention has no centre, the one who is attentive, and so no border.

As long as there's a centre, the 'me', there must be challenge and response, adequate or inadequate, pleasurable or sorrowful. The centre can never be a light to itself; its light is the artificial light of thought and it has many shadows. Compassion is not the shadow of thought but it is light, neither yours nor another's.

The path gradually entered the valley and the stream went by the village to join the sea. But the hills remained changeless and the hoot of an owl was the reply to another. And there was space for silence.

From where one sat on a rock, in an orange orchard, the valley spread out and disappeared into the fold of mountains. It was early in the morning and the shadows were long, soft and open. The quails were calling with their sharp demand and the mourning dove was cooing, with soft, gentle lilt, a sad song so early in the morning. The mocking-bird was making swooping curves in the air, turning somersaults, delighted with the world. A big tarantula, hairy and dark, slowly came out from under the rock, stopped, felt the morning air and un-hurriedly went its way. The orange trees were in long straight lines, acre upon acre, with their bright fruit and fresh blos-som—flower and fruit on the same tree at the same time. The smell of these blossoms was quietly pervasive and with the heat of the sun the smell would get deeper, more insistent. The sky was very blue and soft and all the hills and mountains were still dreaming.

It was a lovely morning, cool and fresh, with that strange beauty which man had not yet destroyed. The lizards came out and sought a warm spot in the sun; they stretched out to get their bellies warm and their long tails turned sideways. It was a happy morning and the soft light covered the land and the endless beauty of life. Meditation is the essence of this beauty, expressed or silent. Expressed, it takes form, substance; silent it's not to be put into word, form or colour. From si-lence, expression, action is beauty and whole, and all struggle, conflict ceases. The lizards were moving into the shade and the humming-birds and the bees were among the blossoms.

Without passion there's no creation. Total abandonment brings this unending passion. Abandonment with a motive is one thing, and without a purpose, without calculation, it is another. That which has an end, a direction, is short lived, becomes mischievous and commercial, vulgar. The other, not driven by any cause, intention or gain, has no beginning and no ending. This abandonment is the emptying of the mind of the 'me', the self. This 'me' can lose itself in some activity, in some comforting belief or fanciful dream but such loss is the continuing of the self in another form, identifying with another ideology and action. The abandonment of the self is not an act of will, for the will is the self. Any movement of the self, horizontally or vertically, in any direction, is still within the field of time and sorrow. Thought may give itself over to something, sane or insane, reasonable or idiotic, but being in its very structure and nature fragmentary, its very enthusiasm, excitement, soon turn into pleasure and fear. In this area the abandonment of the self is illusory, with little meaning. The awareness of all this is the awakening to the activities of the self; in this attention there is no centre, the self. The urge to express oneself for identification is the outcome of confusion and the meaninglessness of existence. To seek a meaning is the beginning of fragmentation; thought can and does give a thousand meanings to life, each one inventing its own meanings which are merely opinions and convictions and there's no end to them. The very living is the whole meaning but when life is a conflict, a struggle, a battlefield of ambition, competition and the worship of success, the search for power and position, then life has no meaning. What is the need of expression?

Does creation lie in the thing produced? The thing produced by hand or by the mind, however beautiful or utilitarian, is it that one is after? Does this self-abandoned passion need expression? When there is a need, a compulsion, is it the passion of creation? As long as there is division between creator and the created, beauty, love, come to an end. You may produce a most excellent thing in colour or in stone, but if your daily life contradicts that supreme excellence—the total abandonment of the self—that which you have produced is for admiration and vulgarity. The very living is the colour, the beauty and its expression. One needs no other.

The shadows were losing their distance and the quails were quiet. There was only the rock, the trees with their blossom and fruit, the lovely hills and the abundant earth.

In the valley of orange orchards, this one was very well looked after—row upon row of young trees, strong and sparkling in the sun. The soil was good, well-watered, manured and cared for. It was a beautiful morning with a clear blue sky, warm and the air was softly pleasant. The quails in the bushes were fussing about, with their sharp calls; a sparrow-hawk was hovering in the air, motionless, and soon it came down to sit on a branch in the next orange tree and went to sleep. It was so close that the sharp claws, the marvellous speckled feathers and the sharp beak were clearly visible; it was within the reach of an arm. It had been earlier in the morning along the avenue of mimosa and the small birds were crying out their alarm. Under the bushes two King snakes, with their dark brown rings along the length of their bodies, were curling around each other, and as they passed close by they were utterly unaware of a human presence. They had been on a shelf in the shed, stretched out, their dark, bright eyes watching and waiting for the mice. They stared without blinking for they had no eyelids. They must have been there during the night and now they were among the bushes. It was their ground and they were seen often, and on picking up one of them, it coiled around the arm and felt cold to the touch. All those living things seemed to have their own order, their own discipline and their own play and gaiety.

Materialism, that nothing exists but matter, is the prevailing and the persistent activity of human beings who are affluent and those who are not. There's a whole block of the world which is dedicated to materialism; the structure of its society is based upon this formula, with all its con-sequences.

The other blocks are also materialistic but some kind of

idealistic principles are accepted when it's convenient and discarded under the name of rationality and necessity. In changing the environment, violently or slowly, revolution or evolution, the behaviour of man is changed according to the culture in which he lives. It is an age-old conflict between those who believe man is matter and those who pursue the spirit. This division has brought such misery, confusion, illusion to man.

Thought is material and all its activity, outer or inner, is materialistic. Thought is measurable and so it is time. Within this area, consciousness is matter. Consciousness is its content; the content is consciousness; they are inseparable. The content is the many things which thought has put together: the past modifying the present which is the future which is time. Time is movement within the area of consciousness, expanded or contracted. Thought is memory, experience and knowledge, and this memory, with its images and its shadows, is the self, the 'me' and the 'not me', the 'we' and 'they'. The essence of division is the self with all its attributes and qualities. Materialism only gives strength and growth to the self. The self may and does identify itself with the State, with an ideology, with activities of the 'non-me', religious or secular, but it is still the self. Its beliefs are self-created, as are its pleasures and fears. Thought by its very nature and structure is fragmentary, and conflict and war are between the various fragments, the nationalities, the races and ideologies. A materialistic humanity will destroy itself unless the self is wholly abandoned. The abandonment of the self is always of primary importance. And only from this revolution a new society can be put together.

The abandonment of the self is love, com-passion: passion for all things—the starving, the suffering, the homeless and for the materialist and the believer. Love is not sentimentality, romanticism; it is as strong and final as death.

Slowly the fog from the sea came over the western hills like huge waves; it folded itself over the hills and down into the valley and it would presently reach up here; it would become cooler with the coming darkness of the night. There would be no stars and there would be complete silence. It is a factual silence and not the silence which thought has cultivated, in which there is no space.

MALIBU *

April 1, 1975

Even so early in the morning the sun was hot and burning. There wasn't a breeze and not a leaf was stirring. In the ancient temple it was cool and pleasant; the bare feet were aware of the solid slabs of rocks, their shapes and their unevenness. Many thousands of people must have walked on them for a thousand years. It was dark there after the glare of the morning sun and in the corridors there seemed to be few people that morning and in the narrow passage it was still darker. This passage led to a wide corridor which led to the inner shrine. There was a strong smell of flowers and the incense of many centuries. And a hundred Brahmanas, freshly bathed, in newly washed white loincloths, were chanting. Sanskrit is a powerful language, resonant with depth. The ancient walls were vibrating, almost shaking to the sound of a hundred voices. The dignity of the sound was incredible and the sacredness of the moment was beyond the words. It was not the words that awakened this immensity but the depth of the sound, the sound of many thousand years held within these walls and in the immeasurable space beyond them. It was not the meaning of those words, nor the clarity of their pronunciation, nor the dark beauty of the temple but the quality of sound that broke walls and the limitations of the human mind. The song of a bird, the distant flute, the breeze among the leaves, all these break down the walls that human beings have created for themselves.

In the great cathedrals and lovely mosques, the chants and the intoning of their sacred books it is the sound that opens the heart, to tears and beauty. Without space there's no beauty; without space you have only walls and measurements; without space there's no depth; without space there's only poverty, inner and outer. You have so little space in your mind; it's so crammed full of words, remembrances, knowledge, experiences and problems. There's hardly any space left, only the everlasting chatter of thought. And so your muse-ums are filled and every shelf with books. Then you fill the places of entertainment, religious or otherwise. Or you build a wall around yourself, a narrow space of mischief and pain. Without space, inner and outer, you become violent and ugly.

Everything needs space to live, to play and to chant. That which is sacred cannot live without space. You have no space when you hold, when there is sorrow, when you become the centre of the universe. The space that you occupy is the space that thought has built around you and that is misery and confusion. The space that thought measures is the division between you and me, we and they. This division is endless pain. There's that solitary tree in a wide, green, open field.

It was not a land of trees, meadows, streams and flowers and mirth. It was a sunburnt land of sand and barren hills, without a single tree or bush; a land of desolation, an endless scorched earth mile upon mile; there wasn't even a bird and not even oil with its derricks and flames of burning oil. Consciousness could not hold the desolation and every hill was a barren shadow. For many hours we flew over this vast emptiness and at last there were snow peaks, forest and streams, villages and spreading towns.

You may have a great deal of knowledge and be vastly poor. The poorer you are the greater the demand for knowledge. You expand your consciousness with great varieties of knowledge, accumulating experiences and remembrances and yet are vastly poor. The skilful use of know-ledge may bring you wealth and give you eminence and power but there may still be poverty. This poverty breeds callousness; you play while the house is burning. This poverty merely strengthens the intellect or gives to the emotions the weakness of sentiment. It's this poverty that brings about imbalance, the lack of harmony, the conflict of division between the outer and inner. There's no knowledge of the inner, only of the outer. The knowledge of the outer informs us erroneously that there must be knowledge of the inner. Self-knowing is brief and shallow; the mind is soon beyond it, like crossing a river. You make a lot of noise in going across the river and to mistake the noise as knowledge of the self is to expand poverty. This expansion of consciousness is the activity of poverty. Religions, culture, knowledge, can in no way enrich this poverty.

The skill of intelligence is to put knowledge in its right place. Without knowledge it's not possible to live in this technological and almost mechanical civilization but it will not transform the human being and his society. Knowledge is not the excellence of intelligence; intelligence can and does use knowledge and thus transforms man and his society. Intelligence is not the mere cultivation of the intellect and its integrity. It comes out of the understanding of the whole consciousness of man, yourself and not a part, a separate segment, of yourself. The study and the understanding of the movement of your own mind and heart give birth to this intelligence. You are the content of your consciousness; in knowing yourself you will know the universe. This knowing is beyond the word for the word is not the thing. The freedom from the known, every minute, is the essence of intelligence. It's this intelligence that is in operation in the universe if you leave it alone. You are destroying this sacredness of order through the ignorance of yourself. This ignorance is not banished by the studies others have made about you or themselves. You yourself have to study the content of your own consciousness. The studies others have made of themselves, and so of yourself, are the descriptions but not the described. The word is not the thing.

Only in relationship can you know yourself, not in abstraction and certainly not in isolation. Even in a monastery you are related to the society which has made the monastery as an escape, or closed the doors to freedom. The movement of behaviour is the sure guide to yourself; it's the mirror of your consciousness; this mirror will re-veal its content, the images, the attachments, the fears, the loneliness, the joy and the sorrow. Poverty lies in running away from this, either in its sublimations or in its identities. Negating without resistance this content of consciousness is the beauty and compassion of intelligence.

How extraordinarily beautiful is the great curve of a wide river. You must see it from a certain height, not too far up or too close as it meanders lazily through the green fields. The river was wide, full of water, blue and clear. We were not flying at a great altitude and we could just see the strong current in the middle of the river with its tiny waves; we followed it, past towns and villages to the sea. Each curve had its own beauty, its own strength, its own movement. And far away were the great snow-covered peaks, pink in the early morning light; they covered the eastern horizon. The wide river and those great mountains seemed to hold, for that hour, eternity—this overwhelming sense of timeless space. Though the plane was rushing south-east, in that space there was no direction, no movement, only that which is. For a whole hour there was nothing else, not even the noise of the jets. Only when the Captain announced that we would soon be landing did that full hour come to an end. There was no memory of that hour, no record of the content of that hour and so thought had no hold on it. When it came to an end there were no remains, the slate was clean again. So thought had no means to cultivate that hour and so it got ready to leave the plane.

What thought thinks about is made into a reality but it's not truth. Beauty can never be the expression of thought. A bird is not made by thought and so it's beautiful. Love is not shaped by thought and when it is it becomes something quite different. The worship of the intellect and its integrity is a reality made by thought. But it is not compassion.

Thought cannot manufacture com-passion; it can make it into a reality, a necessity, and so it can never be compassion. Thought by its very nature is fragmentary and so it lives in a fragmented world of division and conflict. So knowledge is fragmentary and however much it is piled up, layer after layer, it will still remain fragmented, broken up. Thought can put together a thing called integration and that too will be a fragment.

The very word science means knowledge, and man hopes through science he will be transformed into a sane and happy human being. And so man is pursuing eagerly knowledge of all the things of the earth and of himself. Knowledge is not com-passion and without compassion knowledge breeds mischief and untold misery and chaos. Knowledge cannot make man love another; it can create war and the instruments of destruction but cannot bring love to the heart or peace to the mind. To perceive all this is to act, not an action based on memory and patterns. Love is not memory, a remembrance of pleasures.

By chance it happened that one lived alone for some months in a small dilapidated house, high in the mountains, far from other houses. There were lots of trees and as it was spring there was perfume in the air. The solitude was of the mountains and of the beauty of the red earth. The towering peaks were covered with snow and some of the trees were in bloom. One lived alone amidst this splendour. The forest was nearby, with deer, an occasional bear and those big monkeys with black faces and long tails, and of course there were serpents too. In deep solitude in strange ways one was related to them all. One could not hurt a thing, even that white daisy on the path. In that relationship the space between you and them didn't exist; it was not contrived; it was not an intellectual or an emotional conviction that brought this about but simply it was so. A group of those large monkeys would come around, especially in the evening; a few were on the ground but most of them would be sitting in the trees quietly watching. Surprisingly they were still; occasionally there would be a scratch or two and we would watch each other. They would come every evening now, neither too close nor too high among the trees, and we would be silently aware of each other. We had become quite good friends but they didn't want to encroach upon one's solitude. Walking one afternoon in the forest one came suddenly upon them in an open space. There must have been well over thirty of them, young and old, sitting among the trees round the open space, absolutely silent and still. One could have touched them; there was no fear in them and sitting on the ground we watched each other till the sun went behind the peaks.

If you lose touch with nature you lose touch with humanity. If there's no relationship with nature then you become a killer; then you kill baby seals, whales, dolphins and man either for gain, for 'sport', for food or for knowledge. Then nature is frightened of you, withdrawing its beauty. You may take long walks in the woods or camp in lovely places but you are a killer and so lose their friendship. You probably are not related to anything, to your wife or your husband; you are much too busy, gaining and losing, with your own private thoughts, pleasures and pains. You live in your own dark isolation and the escape from it is further darkness. Your interest is in a short survival, mindless, easygoing or violent. And thousands die of hunger or are butchered because of your irresponsibility. You leave the ordering of the world to the lying corrupt politician, to the intellectuals, to the experts. Because you have no integrity, you build a society that's immoral, dishonest, a society based on utter selfishness. And then you escape from all this for which you alone are responsible, to the beaches, to the woods or carry a gun for 'sport'.

You may know all this but knowledge does not bring about transformation in you. You have to act integrally, as a total human being. Then when you have this sense of the whole, you will be related to the universe.

It is not that extraordinary blue of the Mediterranean; the Pacific has an ethereal blue, especially when there is a gentle breeze from the west as you drive north along the coast road. It is so tender, dazzling, clear and full of mirth. Occasionally you would see whales blowing on their way north and rarely their enormous heads as they threw themselves out of the water. There was a whole pod of them, blowing; they must be very powerful animals. That day the sea was a lake, still and utterly quiet, without a single wave; there was not that clear dancing blue. The sea was asleep and you watched it with wonder. The house overlooked the sea*. It is a beautiful house, with a quiet garden, a green lawn and flowers. It's a spacious house with the light of the Californian sun. And rabbits loved it too; they would come early in the morning and late in the evening; they would eat up flowers and the newly planted pansies, marigolds and the small flowering plants. You couldn't keep them out though there was a wire netting all around, and to kill them would be a crime. But a cat and a barn owl brought order to the garden; the black cat wandered about the garden; the owl perched itself during the day among the thick eucalyptus; you could see it, motionless, eyes closed, round and big. The rabbits disappeared and the garden flourished and the blue Pacific flowed effortlessly.

It is only man that brings disorder to the universe. He's ruthless and extremely violent. Wherever he is he brings misery and confusion in himself and in the world about him. He lays waste and destroys and he has no compassion. In himself there is no order and so what he touches becomes soiled and chaotic.

His politics have become a refined gangsterism of power,

deceit, personal or national, group against group. His economy is restricted and so not universal. His society is immoral, in freedom and under tyranny. He is not religious though he believes, worships and goes through endless, meaningless rituals. Why has he become like this—cruel, irresponsible and so utterly self-centred? Why? There are a hundred explanations and those who explain, subtly with words that are born out of knowledge of many books and experiments on animals, are caught in the net of human sorrow, ambition, pride and agony. The description is not the described, the word is not the thing. Is it because he is looking for outward causes, the environment conditioning man, hoping the outer change transforms the inner man? Is it because he's so attached to his senses, dominated by their immediate demands? Is it because he lives so entirely in the movement of thought and knowledge? Or is it because he's so romantic, sentimental, that he becomes ruthless with his ideals, make-belief and pretensions? Is it because he is always led, a follower, or becomes a leader, a guru?

This division as the outer and inner is the beginning of his conflict and misery; he is caught in this contradiction, in this ageless tradition. Caught in this meaningless division, he is lost and becomes a slave to others. The outer and the inner are the imagination and the invention of thought; as thought is fragmentary, it makes for disorder and conflict which is division. Thought cannot bring about order, an effortless flow of virtue. Virtue is not the continuous repetition of memory, practice. Thought-knowledge is time-binding. Thought by its very nature and structure cannot grasp the whole flow of life, as a total movement.

Thought-knowledge cannot have an insight into this wholeness; it cannot be aware of this choicelessly as long as it remains as the perceiver, the outsider looking in. Thought-knowledge has no place in perception. The thinker is the thought; the perceiver is the perceived. Only then is there an effortless movement in our daily life.

Ojai *

In this part of the world it doesn't rain much, about fifteen to twenty inches a year, and these rains are most welcome for it doesn't rain for the rest of the year. There is snow then on the mountains and during summer and autumn they are bare, sunburnt, rocky and forbidding; only in the spring are they mellow and welcoming. There used to be bear, deer, bob cat, quail and any number of rattlers. But now they are disappearing; the dreaded man is encroaching. It had rained for some time now and the valley was green, the orange trees bore fruit and flower. It is a beautiful valley, quiet away from the village, and you heard the mourning dove. The air was slowly being filled with the scent of orange blossoms and in a few days it would be overpowering, with the warm sun and windless days. It was a valley wholly surrounded by hills and mountains; beyond the hills was the sea and beyond the mountains desert. In the summer it would be unbearably hot but there was always beauty here, far from the maddening crowd and their cities. And at night there would be extraordinary silence, rich and penetrating. Cultivated meditation is a sacrilege to beauty, and every leaf and branch spoke of the joy of beauty and the tall dark cypress was silent with it; the gnarled old pepper tree flowed with it.

You cannot, may not, invite joy; if you do it becomes pleasure. Pleasure is the movement of thought and thought may not, can in no way, cultivate joy, and if it pursues that which has been joyous, then it's only a remembrance, a dead thing.

Beauty is never time-binding; it is wholly free of time and

so of culture. It is there when the self is not. The self is put together by time, by the movement of thought, by the known, by the word. In the abandonment of the self, in that total attention, that essence of beauty is there. The letting go of the self is not the calculated action of desire-will. Will is directive and so resistant, divisive, and so breeds conflict. The dissolution of the self is not the evolution of the knowledge of the self; time as a factor does not enter into it at all. There is no way or means to end it. The total inward non-action is the positive attention of beauty.

You have cultivated a vast network of interrelated activities in which you are caught, and your mind, being conditioned by it, operates inwardly in the same manner. Achievement then becomes the most important thing and the fury of that drive is still the skeleton of the self. That is why you follow your guru, your saviour, your beliefs and ideals; faith takes the place of insight, of awareness. There's no need for prayer, for rituals, when the self is not. You fill the empty spaces of the skeleton with knowledge, with images, with meaningless activities and so keep it seemingly alive.

In the quiet stillness of the mind that which is everlasting beauty comes, uninvited, unsought, without the noise of recognition.

In the silence of deep night and in the quiet still morning when the sun is touching the hills, there is a great mystery. It is there in all living things. If you sit quietly under a tree, you would feel the ancient earth with its incomprehensible mystery. On a still night when the stars are clear and close, you would be aware of expanding space and the mysterious order of all things, of the immeasurable and of nothing, of the movement of the dark hills and the hoot of an owl. In that utter silence of the mind this mystery expands without time and space. There's mystery in those ancient temples built with infinite care, with attention which is love. The slender mosques and the great cathedrals lose this shadowy mystery for there is bigotry, dogma and military pomp. The myth that is concealed in the deep layers of the mind is not mysterious; it is romantic, traditional and conditioned. In the secret recesses of the mind, truth has been pushed aside by symbols, words, images; in them there is no mystery, they are the churnings of thought. In knowledge and its action there is wonder, appreciation and delight. But mystery is quite another thing. It is not an experience, to be recognized, stored up and remembered. Experience is the death of that incommunicable mystery; to communicate you need a word, a gesture, a look, but to be in communion with that, the mind, the whole of you, must be at the same level, at the same time, with the same intensity as that which is called mysterious. This is love. With this the whole mystery of the universe is open.

This morning there wasn't a cloud in the sky, the sun was in the valley and all things were rejoicing, except man.

When he's forced to look, he tears to pieces what he sees, which he calls analysis, runs away from it or doesn't want to see. In the art of seeing lies the miracle of trans-formation, the transformation of 'what is'. The 'what should be' never is. There's vast mystery in the act of seeing. This needs care, attention, which is love.

A very large serpent was crossing a wide cart road just ahead of you, fat, heavy, moving lazily; it was coming from a largish pond a little way off. It was almost black and the light of the evening sun falling on it gave to its skin a high polish. It moved in a leisurely way with lordly dignity of power. It was unaware of you as you stood quietly watching; you were quite close to it; it must have measured well over five feet and it was bulging with what it had eaten. It went over a mound and you walked towards it, looking down upon it a few inches away, its forked black tongue darting in and out; it was moving towards a large hole. You could have touched it for it had a strange attractive beauty. A villager was passing by and called out to leave it alone because it was a cobra. The next day the villagers had put there on the mound a saucer of milk and some hibiscus flowers. On that same road further along there was a bush, high and almost leafless, that had thorns almost two inches long, sharp, greyish, and no animal would dare to touch its succulent leaves. It was protecting itself and woe to anyone that touched it. There were deer there in those woods, shy but very curious; they would allow themselves to be approached but not too close and if you did they would dart away and disappear among the undergrowth. There was one that would let you come quite close, if you were alone, bright-eyed with its large ears forward. They all had white spots on a russet-brown skin; they were shy, gentle and ever-watchful and it was pleasant to be among them. There was a completely white one, which must have been a freak.

The good is not the opposite of the evil. It has never been touched by that which is evil, though it is surrounded by it. Evil cannot hurt the good but the good may appear to do harm and so evil gets more cunning, more mischievous. It can be cultivated, sharpened, expansively violent; it is born within the movement of time, nurtured and skilfully used. But goodness is not of time; it can in no way be cultivated or nurtured by thought; its action is not visible; it has no cause and so no effect. Evil cannot become good for that which is good is not the product of thought; it lies beyond thought, like beauty. The thing that thought produces, thought can undo but it is not the good; as it is not of time, the good has no abiding place. Where the good is, there is order, not the order of authority, punishment and reward; this order is essential, for otherwise society destroys itself and man becomes evil, murderous, corrupt and degenerate. For man is society; they are inseparable. The law of the good is everlasting, unchanging and timeless. Stability is its nature and so it is utterly secure. There is no other security.

Space is order. Space is time, length, width and volume. This morning the sea and the heavens are immense; the horizon where those yellow flowered hills meet the distant sea is the order of earth and heaven; it is cosmic. That cypress, tall, dark, alone, has the order of beauty and the distant house on that wooded hill follows the movement of the mountains that tower over the low-lying hills; the green field with a single cow is beyond time. And the man coming up the hill is held within the narrow space of his problems.

There is a space of nothingness whose volume is not bound by time, the measure of thought. This space the mind cannot enter; it can only observe. In this observation there is no experiencer. This observer has no history, no association, no myth, and so the observer is that which is. Knowledge is extensive but it has no space, for by its very weight and volume it perverts and smothers that space. There is no knowledge of the self, higher or lower; there's only a verbal structure of the self, a skeleton, covered over by thought. Thought cannot penetrate its own structure; what it has put together thought cannot deny and when it does deny, it is the refusal of further gain. When the time of the self is not, the space that has no measure is.

This measure is the movement of reward and punishment, gain or loss, the activity of comparison and conformity, of respectability and the very denial of it. This movement is time, the future with its hope and the attachment which is the past. This complex network is the very structure of the self and its union with the supreme being or the ultimate principle is still within its own field. All this is the activity of thought. Thought can in no way penetrate that space of no time, do what it will. The very method, the curriculum, the practice that thought has invented are not the keys that will open the door, for there is no door, no key. Thought can only be aware of its own endless activity, its own capacity to corrupt, its own deceits and illusions. It is the observer and the observed. Its gods are its own projections and the worship of them is the worship of yourself. What lies beyond thought, beyond the known, may not be imagined or made a myth of or made a secret for the few. It is there for you to see.

MALIBU *

April 23, 1975

The wide river was still as a mill-pond. There wasn't a ripple and the morning breeze hadn't awakened yet for it was early. The stars were in the water, clear and sparkling and the morning star was the brightest. The trees across the river were dark and the village amongst them still slept. There was not a leaf stirring and those small screech owls were rattling away on the old tamarind tree; it was their home and when the sun was on those branches they would be warming themselves. The noisy green parrots were quiet too. All things, even the insects and the cicadas, were waiting, breathless for the sun, in adoration. The river was motionless and the usual small boats with their dark lamps were absent. Gradually over the dark mysterious trees there began the early light of dawn. Every living thing was still in the mystery of that moment; it was the timeless moment of meditation. Your own mind was timeless, without measure; there was no yardstick to measure how long that moment lasted. Only there was a stirring and an awakening, the parrots and the owls, the crows and the mynah, the dogs and a voice across the river. And suddenly the sun was just over the trees, golden and hidden by the leaves. Now the great river was awake, moving; time, length, width and volume were flowing and all life began which never ended.

How lovely it was that morning, the purity of light and the golden path the sun made on those living waters. You were the world, the cosmos, the deathless beauty and the joy of compassion. Only you weren't there; if you were all this would not be.

You bring in the beginning and the ending, to begin again in an endless chain.

In becoming there is uncertainty and in-stability. In nothingness there is absolute stability and so clarity. That which is wholly stable never dies; corruption is in becoming. The world is bent on becoming, achieving, gaining and so there is fear of losing and dying. The mind must go through that small hole which it has put together, the self, to come upon this vast nothingness whose stability thought cannot measure. Thought desires to capture it, use it, cultivate it and put it on the market. It must be made acceptable and so respectable, to be worshipped. Thought cannot put it into any category and so it must be a delusion and a snare; or it must be for the few, for the select. And so thought goes about its own mischievous ways, frightened, cruel, vain and never stable, though its conceit asserts there is stability in its actions, in its exploration, in knowledge it has accumulated. The dream becomes a reality which it has nurtured. What thought has made real is not truth. Nothingness is not a reality but it is the truth. The small hole, the self, is the reality of thought, the skeleton on which it has built all its existence—the reality of its fragmentation, the pain, the sorrow and its love. The reality of its gods or its one god is the careful structure of thought, its prayer, its rituals, its romantic worship. In reality there is no stability or pure clarity.

The knowledge of the self is time, length, width and volume; it can be accumulated, used as a ladder to become, to improve, to achieve. This knowledge will in no way free the mind of the burden of its own reality. You are the burden; the truth of it lies in the seeing of it and that freedom is not the reality of thought. The seeing is the doing. The doing comes from the stability, clarity of nothingness.

Every living thing has its own sensitivity, its own way of life, its own consciousness, but man assumes that his own is far superior and thereby he loses his love, his dignity and becomes insensitive, callous and destructive. In the valley of orange trees, with their fruit and spring blossom, it was a lovely clear morning. The mountains to the north had a sprinkling of snow on them; they were bare, hard and aloof, but against the tender blue sky of early morning they were very close, you could almost touch them. They had that immense sense of age and indestructible majesty and that beauty that comes with timeless grandeur. It was a very still morning and the smell of orange blossom filled the air, the wonder and the beauty of light. The light of this part of the world has a special quality, penetrating, alive and filling the eyes; it seemed to enter into your whole consciousness, sweeping away any dark corners. There was great joy in that and every leaf and blade of grass were rejoicing in it. And the blue jay was hopping from branch to branch and not screeching its head off for a change. It was a lovely morning of light and great depth.

Time has bred consciousness with its content. It is the culture of time. Its content makes up consciousness; without it, consciousness, as we know it, is not. Then there is nothing. We move the little pieces in this consciousness from one area to another according to the pressure of reason and circumstance but in the same field of pain, sorrow and knowledge. This movement is time, the thought and the measure. It is a senseless game that most play, the worthy and the foolish; it is a game of hide and seek with yourself, the shadow and substance of thought, the past and the future of thought. Thought cannot hold this moment, for this moment is not of time. This moment is the ending of time; time has stopped at that moment, there is no movement at that moment and so it is not related to another moment. It has no cause and so no beginning and no end. Consciousness cannot contain it. In that moment of nothingness everything is. Meditation is the emptying of consciousness of its content.

Information about Brockwood Park

Krishnamurti Foundation Trust
Tel: +44 (0) 1962 771 525   Fax: +44 (0) 1962 771 159
E-mail:kft@brockwood.org.uk
Website: www.kfoundation.org

The Krishnamurti Foundation Trust exists to preserve archives of
J. Krishnamurti's teachings and to make them known through books, audio and
video tapes, and other media.

Brockwood Park School
Tel: +44 (0) 1962 771 744   Fax: +44 (0) 1962 771 875
E-mail: admin@brockwood.org.uk
Website: www.brockwood.org.uk

Brockwood Park School, founded by J. Krishnamurti, is an international
co-educational boarding school in the southern English countryside.

It offers a diverse and personalised programme of study for some 60 students aged 13
to 19, providing an education that encourages academic excellence, self-understanding,
creativity and integrity in a safe, non-competitive environment.

The aim is to explore life in the light of J. Krishnamurti's teaching on the transformation
of human consciousness.

The Krishnamurti Study Centre
Tel: +44 (0) 1962 771 748   Fax: +44 (0) 1962 771 755
E-mail: kcentre@brockwood.org.uk
Website: www.brockwood.org.uk/centre

An oasis of quiet, situated in the southern English countryside, the Centre is a place
where adults can stay to study and discuss the teachings of J. Krishnamurti.

The address for all three:
Brockwood Park, Bramdean, Hampshire, SO24 0LQ, England